Sculpture, Monuments and Open Space

Vol. 73. No. 1
Spring 2024

Art in Urban Spaces

Sculpture, Monuments and Open Space

Overview

Sculture, Monuments & Open Space (known previously as Sculpture Review) is dedicated to the advancement, development and appreciation of realist sculpture. Our objective is to show the various ways in which sculptors worldwide and throughout time have worked to express themselves in various media.

Indexing Information

- Art & Architecture Complete (EBSCO Publishing)
- Art & Architecture Source (EBSCO Publishing)
- Arts & Humanities Citation Index (Clarivate Analytics)
- Art Full Text (EBSCO Publishing)
- Art Index/Abstracts (EBSCO Publishing)
- Current Contents: Arts & Humanities (Clarivate Analytics)

About the Policy Studies Organization

The Policy Studies Organization (PSO) is a publisher of academic journals and books, sponsor of conferences, and producer of programs. It seeks to disseminate scholarship and information to serve those making and evaluating policy. It was founded to serve those in a variety of fields who were interested in how public policy and organizational policy were being studied and discussed.

The PSO includes senior executives, undergraduate and graduate students, state legislators, architects, judges, military officers, environmentalists who want to "green" decision making, NGO executives who worry about the future of volunteerism, professors who are working on curriculum revision, government officials in numerous agencies — in short, PSO is for intellectually active people of all persuasions.

For more information: ipsonet.org

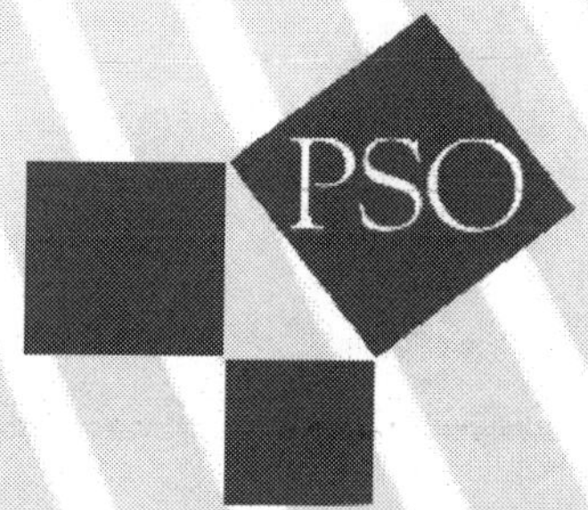

1527 New Hampshire Ave NW
Washington, DC 20036

DOI: 10.1002/smo3.12002

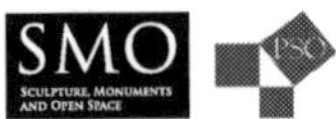

EDITORIAL

Sculpture, monuments and open space—An expanding point of view

The newly titled *Sculpture, Monuments and Open Space*, formerly *Sculpture Review*, is a name that more accurately describes the expanded content the journal has pursued in its most recent issues. *Sculpture Review*, which was started over a half a century ago, was a small black and white printed journal that primarily featured the sculpture of the leading members of the National Sculpture Society (NSS). Over the decades that followed, it continued to expand, and more than doubled in size, eventually adding color and advertising. It also continued to expand its focus to include a wider range of topics with more in-depth views on the sculpture world. This occasionally included entire issues devoted to single topics, such as ceramic sculpture, paper sculpture, the metallic arts, public monuments and a sophisticated range of urban design projects.

About 6 years ago, as the membership of the NSS continued to significantly drop to roughly 1000 active members, the Board was concerned that *Sculpture Review* was becoming a financial burden for the organization, as it was one of its largest line items on the budget. Contending that *Sculpture Review* might be threatening the financial health of the organization, the Board called a special meeting to discuss the potential future of the journal. At this meeting, there were several possible solutions suggested, including the elimination of the journal altogether, or the possibility of publishing a single annual journal featuring the sculpture members of the society.

During this period of discussion and decision making, the Policy Studies Organization (PSO), which has well over two dozen journals, offered to take *Sculpture Review*. And in a mutual agreement, a proposal was designed for a 5-year arrangement between PSO and NSS in an effort to ensure the continued publication of *Sculpture Review*. PSO would openly coordinate with NSS primarily through its editorial committee, made-up of society members, along with new editors to publish *Sculpture Review* and distribute the journal. During this new relationship, the journal was able to continue to expand its focus, including adding a range of new topics and subjects.

A significant benefit of this new arrangement allowed for *Sculpture Review* to be included in the bundles PSO was negotiating along with Sage Publishers to place the journal in thousands of new sites internationally. As bundling is the primary mechanism that magazines and journals are distributed, it offered extensive new possibilities for *Sculpture Review* to be made available in thousands of new sites. Since these bundles are generally negotiated for periods of 5–7 years, *Sculpture Review* was able to be added to new bundles as they were being formed.

In a new arrangement, this first issue of *Sculpture, Monuments and Open Space* has been included in a new partnership that PSO has entered with Wiley Publishing, whose international reach will even more dramatically increase the journal's distribution. This will include a greater number of libraries, universities, and of other designated outlets internationally that will receive this newly branded publication. This will also include thousands of sites in lesser privileged nations such as Sierra Leone and Chad, who receive the bundles free of charge. This newly renamed journal will also have an even greater opportunity to grow in influence and to expand its view to include more in-depth coverage on sculpture, public monuments, and public and urban spaces worldwide.

Gordon Alt,
Editor of Sculpture, Monuments and Open Space Journal

Received: 30 May 2024 | Revised: 7 June 2024 | Accepted: 10 June 2024
DOI: 10.1002/smo3.12004

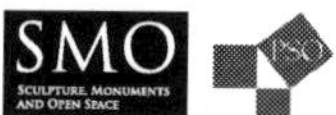

ARTICLE

Why discussion of sculptures and monuments is sadly outdated

Yingjie Wu[1] | **Paul Rich**[2]

[1]Policy Studies Organization, Stuttgart, Germany

[2]Policy Studies Organization, Washington, District of Columbia, USA

Correspondence
Yingjie Wu, Policy Studies Organization, Stuttgart, Germany.
Email: yingjie_wu_andy@163.com

Abstract
This article explores the evolving discourses on sculptures, monuments and open space, under the context of recent changes in the world that influence people's perception of public artworks, shifting from original artistic appreciation to increasingly intense socio-political scrutiny. It considers multiple statues of importance, which were erected, admired, or disdained by the public. This article calls for an urgent need to take inclusive approaches to the representation of artworks in public space that honor women and minorities. Potential solutions are explored, including relocating controversial statues to places of less centrality, adding explanatory plaques, and considering virtual sculptures to preserve open spaces. This article acknowledges that history is not always static and that there's an ongoing trend that artworks in public are placed to inspire new meanings. It contributes to the critical discussion of how art should be and in what way can artworks influence people's perceptions over time.

KEYWORDS
art, change, monument, open space, sculpture

Nothing new under the sun does not entirely ring true in the case of this inaugural *Sculpture, Monuments and Open Space*. *Sculpture Review*, of which this new version is the newest iteration, really dates to the publications of the newly organized National Sculpture Society in the 1890s and to its recent format launched in 1951. In a series of articles, we plan to explore the vast sea changes that the subject faces.

An excellent example of the somewhat sometimes unnoticed centrality of public sculptures and monuments having pride of place in our shared lives was the statue of Athena in the Parthenon (Figure 1). Athena was evidently clad with gold ornaments that doubled as a sort of Fort Knox or Federal Reserve Bank for the Greeks. At any rate, it has been a fairly universal practice to erect almost innumerable sculptures to honor individuals and events that in time became anonymous features of the landscape. We have hurried past things that, when they were erected, were viewed with great affection and attention.

No more. This relative obscurity now has faded as the glare of scrutiny has engendered bitter and continuing controversy. Polite patter about the artistic value is being engulfed by exhaustive examination of the political and social value of what used to be more attractive to pigeons than to people. All of this might surprise those not in academia. It is a reminder that history is not any more a settled matter than medicine or physics. Columbus didn't discover America, and George Washington owned many slaves. What was erected and once faded quietly into the landscape is now as contentious as the latest election.

As a good example, in the case of the Civil War, or if you will, the War Between the States, fondly commemorated in America's South with soldiers on every courthouse law, the noble of losing causes is now viewed with passionate disdain. The removal of glorifying monuments has become a cause as much as school desegregation. The melting pot rather than wreaths has arrived (Figure 2).

This has much to do with the quite justifiable demands of what were sublimated minorities to have their proper place in the nation's chronicle. America has always boasted of its diversity, but now the actual

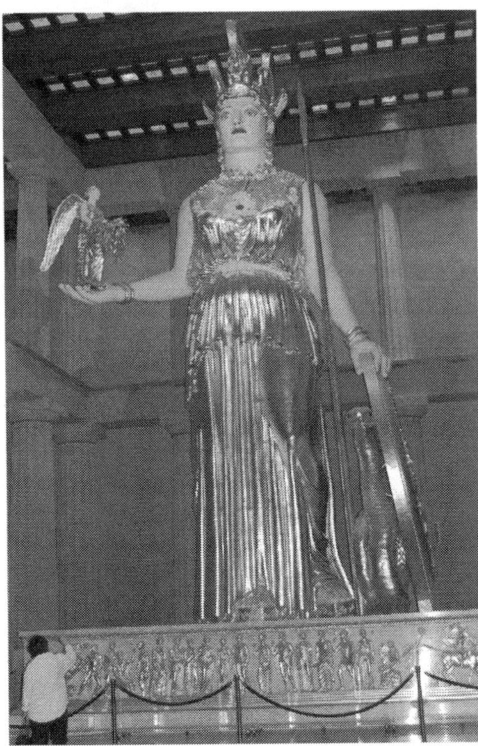

FIGURE 1 Athena at Parthenon in Nashville, TN, USA. Credit: Bubba73 (Jud McCranie), CC BY-SA 4.0, via Wikimedia Commons.

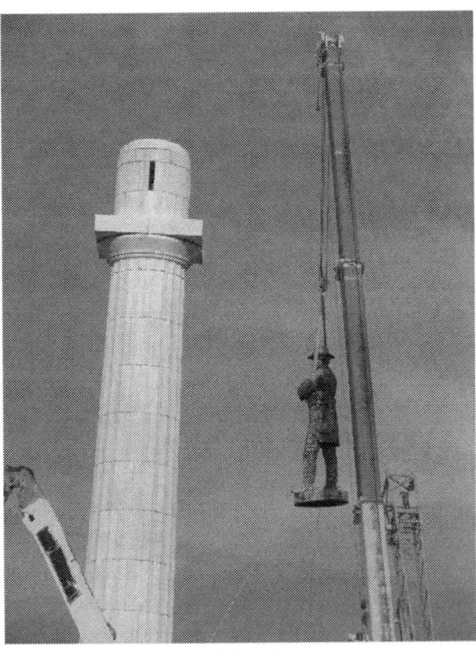

FIGURE 2 Robert E. Lee statue at Lee Circle, New Orleans being removed from atop the column. Credit: Infrogmation of New Orleans, CC BY-SA 4.0, via Wikimedia Commons.

hypocrisy is being examined in terms of the artifacts. Where are the women, the blacks, and the so-called minorities that in fact are the majority? Surely, public space does mean public, not the space of Confederate

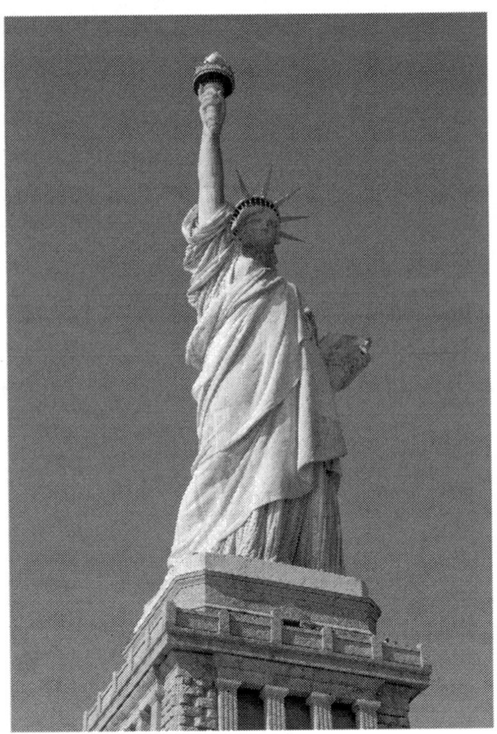

FIGURE 3 Statue of Liberty, New York City. Credit: Jakub Hałun, CC BY 4.0, via Wikimedia Commons.

generals. We need more Statues of Liberty (Figure 3). Some statues are as resented as were Whites-only drinking fountains.

There is a question that the debate raises about how animosities can be abated, and divisions healed. An answer might be to add more rather than junking what we now have. For example, we need more monuments dedicated to women. But the criticisms are valid, and something needs to be done. The Confederates on courthouse lawns are in the ways of thinking of many, not about heroism but about racism and White supremacy. The same applies of course to statues like those of Cecil Rhodes (Figure 4), which recall not the glories of the Empire but tales of repression. However, in fairness, aren't the pyramids a monument to the slaves of the ancient Egypt? Where does the revisionism cease? Isn't it impractical to change everything? What do we do about how slavery helped build the White House? Should we rid ourselves of the Jefferson Memorial because Thomas Jefferson owned slaves (Figure 5)? The same question could be asked about the Christopher Columbus statues, which are seen by many as symbols of colonialism and the suffering of indigenous peoples. Likewise, should we reconsider the legacy of Winston Churchill, who, despite his role in World War II, made statements that many find deeply problematic today? The list of such examples can go on and on.

This of course leads to the larger question of the use of public space. Is it sane for municipalities to maintain golf courses, which are limited in the number of people who can use them and enormously wasteful of water? As for sculptures, would benches to sit on be more welcome and a better memorial than a bronze bust?

Our notions of what is right and what is wrong do change. Gay marriage is now accepted by the majority of Americans. Marijuana is legitimized, and stores selling it are paying billions in taxes. But not everyone likes those changes and is on the merry-go-round of change. The process of removing or altering troubles artists and they certainly know that their work is not safe. Quite suddenly, their creations run into unexpected challenges. Their experiments are condemned. Your good taste is my abhorrence.

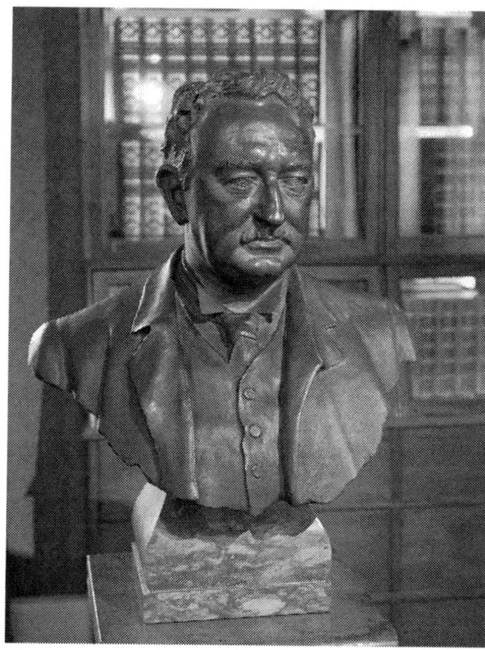

FIGURE 4 A late 19th-century portrait bust of Cecil Rhodes at a public museum in Hertfordshire, England. Credit: Acabashi, CC BY-SA 4.0, via Wikimedia Commons.

The view that sculpture should be realistic has been the war cry of the National Sculpture Society, and one has to sympathize with the view that sharks suspended in formaldehyde are not everyone's idea of art. We are at a critical moment and in the coming issues of this journal we certainly play a role in the debate. The curse that may you live in interesting times has become a reality.

The Statue of Liberty, that of Athena in Nashville, of Vulcan in Birmingham, Alabama (Figure 6), are examples of how large numbers of people can, if given an opportunity, relate to art, and of how the setting is so crucial.[1] Sculpture itself is highly dependent on its setting, a simple point which has been missed in much modern commentary and which has a direct relationship to how space is used. The Kinfolk Foundation co-founder Idris Brewster comments about its unique efforts to redress the setting challenges by creating digital sculptures and, "He believes that in a nation where there are ten times as many monuments honoring mermaids as honoring U.S. congresswomen, and where statues of Robert E. Lee outnumber those of Frederick Douglas, having more diverse monuments makes more sense."[2] The same motivations have led

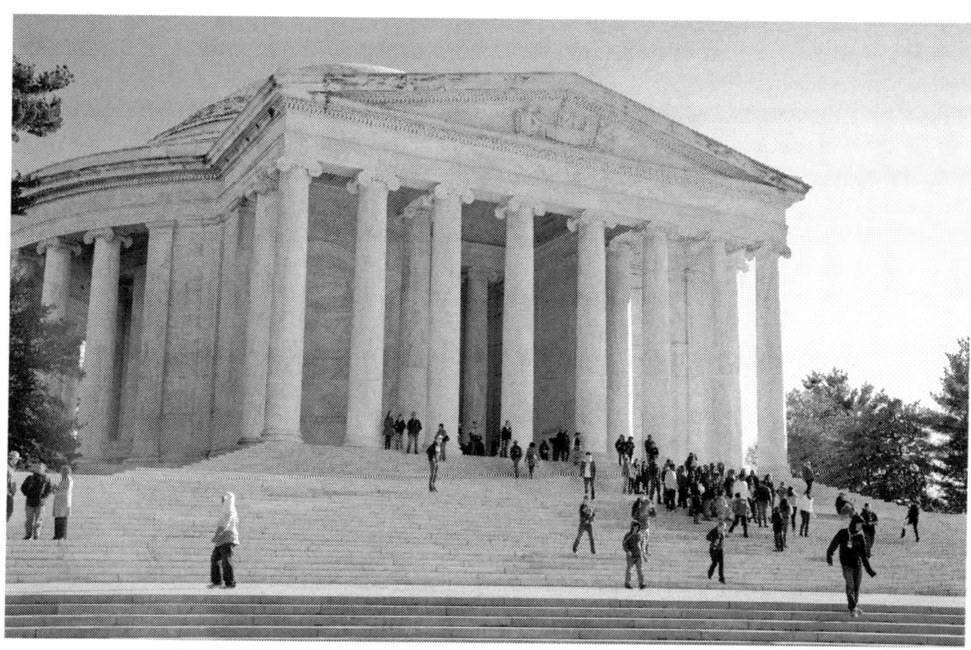

FIGURE 5 The Thomas Jefferson Memorial is a presidential memorial in Washington, DC dedicated to Thomas Jefferson, an American Founding Father and the third President of the United States. Credit: Michael Silva, CC BY-SA 2.0, via Wikimedia Commons.

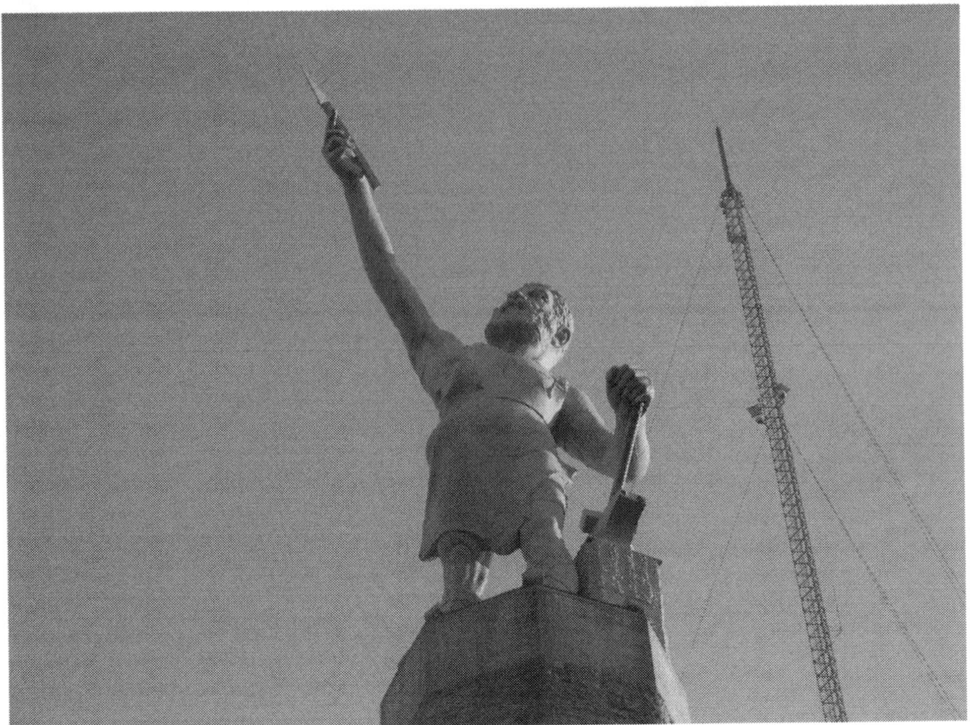

FIGURE 6 Vulcan, the largest cast iron statue in the world, located in Birmingham, AL. Credit: Tepp01, CC BY-SA 4.0, via Wikimedia Commons.

to the sculptures placed by protest groups along Mexico City's famous Reforma boulevard: Christopher Columbus is gone and in its place is a woman with raised fist. The new Reforma sculptures are rallying points for demands for action and redress. According to a recent article from Washington Post, "Activists have installed anti-monuments up and down Reforma, as well as in nearby plazas. The sculptures protest government repression, deaths blamed on bureaucratic or corporate indifference, pervasive violence against women in a machista culture."[3] Alexandra Délano, a scholar at the New School in New York, said activists "are trying to create a space where memory does not mean closure." Instead, she said, "memory means continuous struggle."[3]

Open space can benefit from art, and there are innumerable examples where art adds value. A relatively small space acquires a focus on the placing of an appropriate sculpture. An excellent much-photographed example is Overbeck's Garden at Sharpitor, Devon, featuring The Lark's First Flight, bronze, by Albert Bruce-Joy (Figure 7). It provides just the right accent to the lush surroundings and is the inevitable gathering place for visitors. Charlotte Mullins writes, "In her left hand, she holds a tiny lark's nest with baby birds clustered inside. It seems as if she has just released one of the clutches into the sky for its first adventure."[4]

The meaning? Perhaps the act of releasing the bird is a statement, but the meaning can be even more plain. Meaning can be very explicit. For its 50th anniversary, NASA commissioned the "worm," the highly stylized letters of its name.[5] Sculptors like Misha Japabwaia have created body casts, including pregnant women's bellies. C. J. Munn's commission for the jeweler Susi Smither is "... a torso sculpture is dark blue with abstract symbols, and I intended to evoke the magic of birth."[6] However, should sculptures always have meanings? Not always, according to Do Ho Suh, who has created what he calls a "counter-monument," an empty pedestal held up by little men and women, that now sits in front of the National Museum of Asian Art in Washington. It is an empty pedestal in a city of many pedestals, and perhaps asks us if they have the meanings that were originally intended.[7]

The seriousness of the current controversies about sculptures and monuments should not be understated. It emphasizes the responsibility to discuss these issues in an arts journal such as this. A head-in-the-sand approach, prattling about the sculpture and not its environment is indefensible when for some the Confederate commemorations of the "Lost Cause" are daily vivid reminders of the days of Jim Crow, the Ku Klux Klan and school segregation. In 2017, the statue of Robert E. Lee in Charlottesville, Virginia, was central to confrontations resulting in the death of a protester (Figure 8). When the University of North Carolina removed a Confederate memorial, deep divisions were created among the alumni. The removal

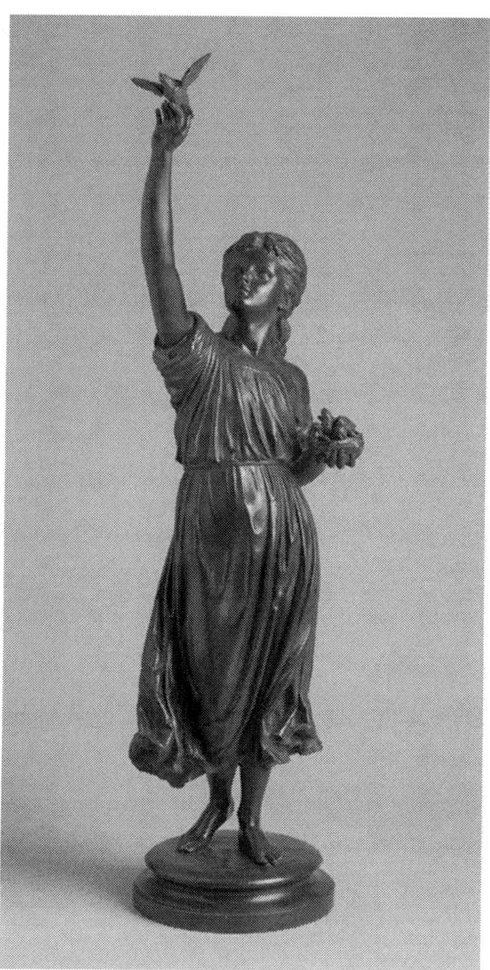

FIGURE 7 The Lark's First Flight, artwork in Aberdeen Archives, Gallery & Museums Collection. Credit: Albert Bruce-Joy, Public domain, via Wikimedia Commons.

of statues in New Orleans has similarly created unhealed wounds.

Indigenous peoples, who were in the millions when Columbus "discovered" America, have occupied the continent for thousands of years and built impressive communities long before his voyages. Indigenous groups have been busy raising objections to their treatment in the arts, as well as defending open space which is sacred to them without embellishments. Noteworthy has been the work of Cannupa Hanska Luger of the Standing Rock Reservation in North Dakota. The near extinction of bison by Europeans deprived tribes of their livings and so understandable is his work recently unveiled in New York City called *Attrition*. A steel buffalo is planted in grasses native to its Plains environment, near City Hall.[*]

Of course, the debate over sculptures and monuments is closely related to the revisionist controversies about other commemorations such as the names of buildings. Harvard has been so concerned about this that it has created a special Committee to Articulate Principles on Renaming. Among the problems are the names of residential Harvard houses such as Winthrop, named for a family that owned slaves.[†] The Harvard Law School dropped its longstanding insignia because it was that of a slave owner.

The maxim that one is either part of the problem or part of the solution applies. There is an obligation rather than shouting fire to suggest solutions that might calm matters. One obvious approach is to move the sculptures and monuments to less central locations such as cemeteries. Another is to place alternatives nearby, or at least explanatory plaques. The less constructive solution, i.e., the destruction of the offending objects, can be regarded as an assault on history. But clearly, some sculptures and monuments are intolerable, such as the Nazi swastika. This journal will be discussing alternatives to the melting pot. One is to attach online files to every sculpture and monuments that explain their history and significance, activated by phones so anyone can access the information on site or afar. We will be actively promoting this and sponsoring projects.

The scramble to create sculptures and memorials to counteract the moral and ethical problems of the current ones has engendered bitterness and divisiveness. An example has been the rocky road travelled by the Harvard proposal to create a memorial to the enslaved who contributed to Harvard's foundation and early days. The faculty chairs of the project have resigned, alleging pressure to hurry.[‡] A solution may be to pursue virtual monuments that can be augmented or changed. Moreover, virtual sculptures and monuments do not consume or interfere with open space.

Open space can be preserved by applying technology. It does not have to be violated by permanent installations. An example of the progress being made in this direction is the Price Sculpture Forest, a nature preserve in Coupeville, Washington state, which invites artists around the world to participate in an augmented reality exhibition of real-world sculptures:

"Your real-world physical sculpture will be digitally transformed for onsite display ... A custom Augmented Reality phone app has been created specifically for this exhibition at Price Sculpture Forest. Visitors will download the app onsite (free WiFi is provided) and be able to view your sculpture via a QR code on your sculpture plaque that shows your name and sculpture title. The visitors can then see your high-resolution sculpture on

*info@publicartfund.org.

†See https://www.harvardmagazine.com/2024/05/harvard-dename-winthrop-house?utm_source=email&utm_medium=newsletter&utm_term=weekly&utm_content=dename-winthrop&utm_campaign=053124.

‡https://www.thecrimson.com/article/2024/6/1/harvard-legacy-of-slavery-resignation-letter/.

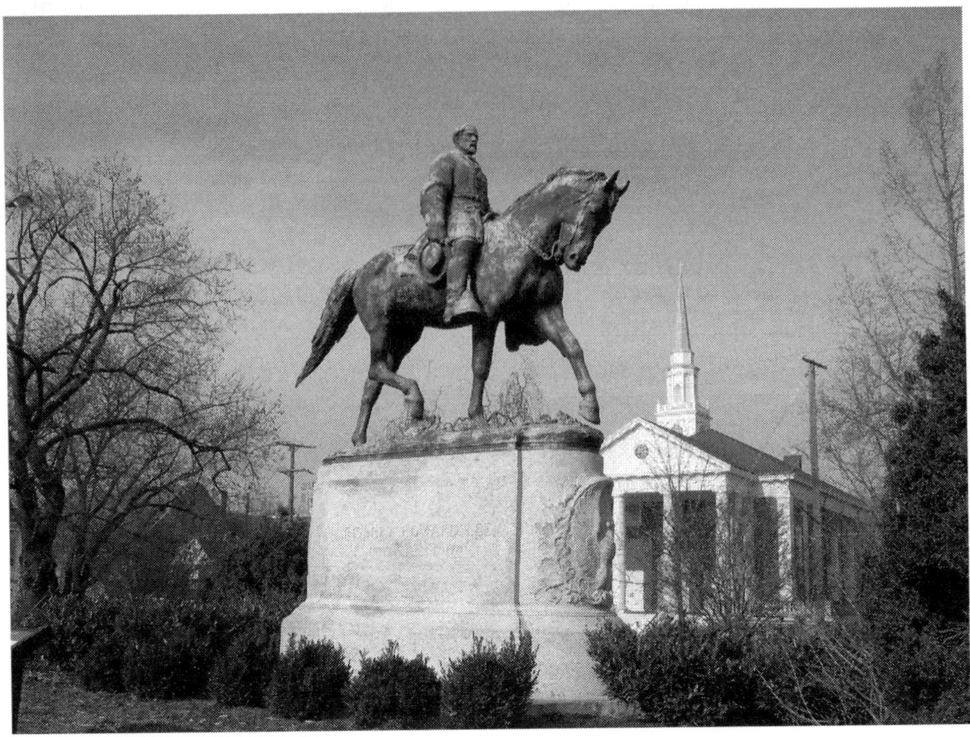

FIGURE 8 Lee Park, named after General Robert Edward Lee, Charlottesville, VA. Credit: Cville dog, Public domain, via Wikimedia Commons.

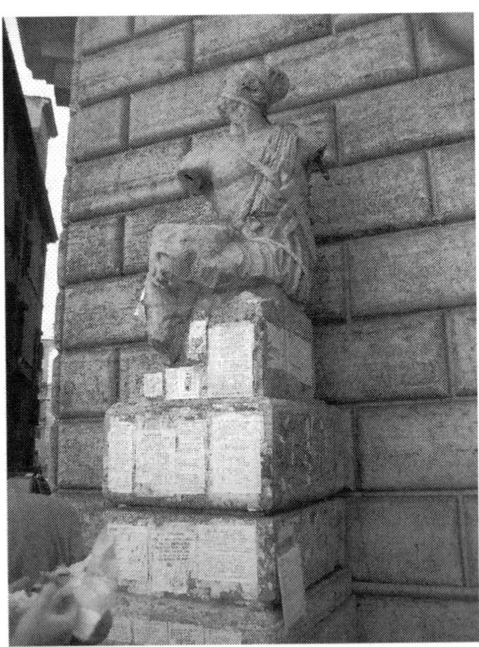

FIGURE 9 Pasquino (one of the talking statues) in Piazza Pasquino, behind Piazza Navona, Rome. Credit: Lalupa, Public domain, via Wikimedia Commons.

the pedestal seamlessly placed within the visual context of the entire area, background, and people there. They can walk around your sculpture to see it from all angles and view it up close or from a distance. They can even stand by your sculpture and take a picture with it."[§]

The idea of "talking statues" is not a product of computer chips but actually goes back to centuries ago. In Rome, during the Renaissance, people wrote their social criticisms and left them on sculptures. They were called the statues parlanti, or talking statues. Perhaps most important was *Pasquino*, a sculpture of a Greek hero and near the important buildings (Figure 9). There were and are a number of others. Pasquinades, as the messages were called, tacked on the sculptures, gave voice about topics that otherwise would have been suppressed. Remarkably, they are still in use, plastered with the latest barbs aimed at politicians and popes. So, attaching virtual sites to sculptures and monuments is in its way simply a refinement of something Romans have enjoyed for centuries.

REFERENCES

1 Renki, Margaret. 2024. "A Tiny Museum Shows the Way Forward." *New York Times* A22, May 28, 2024.
2 Iscoe, Adam. 2023. "Invisible Monuments." *The New Yorker* 9, November 27, 2023.
3 Sheridan, Mary Beth, and Luis Antonio Rojas. 2024. "Underground Anti-Monument Movement Brings Painful History to Mexico City." *Washington Post* 1, February 27, 2024. https://www.washingtonpost.com/world/2024/02/27/mexico-antimonuments-paseo-reforma/

[§]https://sculptureforest.org/.

4 Mullins, Charlotte. 2024. “The Lark's First Flight.” *Country Life*, 54 April 10, 2024.
5 Sullivan, Rober. 2023. “A Design Geek's Space Race: Meatball vs. Worm.” *The New Yorker* 8, November 27, 2023.
6 Ellwood, Mark. 2024. “All Shapes and Forms.” *Washington Post* C2, May 27, 2024.
7 Capps, Kriston. 2024. “He's Turning Public Art Upside Down.” *Washington Post* 12, May 3, 2024.

DOI: 10.1002/smo3.12006

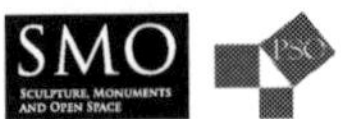

ARTICLE

The Cavanaugh Walk, a unique urban art treasure

Gordon J. Alt

John Cavanaugh Foundation, Washington, District of Columbia, USA

Correspondence
Gordon J. Alt
Email: gordonalt23@gmail.com

KEYWORDS
art, artist, Cavanaugh, Cavanaugh Walk, Dupont Circle, sculpture

The Cavanaugh Walk is both a unique, as well as a dynamic urban art project, some of which is already in place and part of it is currently being implemented in the Dupont Circle neighborhood in Washington, DC. This neighborhood, which is adjacent to the White House and Lafayette Park, is the most active destination for visitors to the city, after visiting the nationally important monuments and other national historic sites as well as the National Mall (Figure 1). This cultural project centers on the public sculpture of nationally recognized artist John Cavanaugh. Cavanaugh did not only reside in the DuPont Circle neighborhood and established his studio there, but he was also an active contributor to the growth and renewal of the DuPont neighborhood. While several of his public sculptures have already been placed in a number of states around the country, the majority of his public sculpture has been installed in Washington, DC. This also includes over a dozen of his works that have already been placed in the Dupont Circle neighborhood (Figure 2).

In 2017, four additional Cavanaugh sculptures were installed in a newly created sculpture garden on the grounds of the former Whittemore Mansion, which houses the headquarters of the Women's National Democratic Club. This new sculpture park is less than a block from the Dupont Circle Fountain, and it is also on the Q Street side of the mansion which is one of the busiest arteries in the neighborhood. The newly installed sculpture represents the four stages in a woman's life from childhood to old age (Figure 3). There was also another Cavanaugh sculpture installed at the same time which was of the powerful Congresswoman from New York, Bella Abzug, which was placed on a pedestal in the entry foyer.

This installation of his work was an important success for both residents of the neighborhood and the many visiting tourists who come to the DuPont Circle area. Both the leadership of the Public Studies Organization, whose headquarters building was across the street from the sculpture park and were pivotal in supporting the park, along with the John Cavanaugh Foundation, which developed and installed the project, were very pleased with Its success. And because of the hype and activity seen constantly around the new installation, it was proposed that additional Cavanaugh sculptures could successfully be placed in nearby sites and create a significant visual connection throughout the neighborhood. An effort could be made to extend the Cavanaugh sculptures to form the basis of the Walk (Figure 4).

Well-designed informational kiosks could be placed near the metro exits and in Dupont Circle Park and the Cavanaugh sculpture could then act as the markers that could lead visitors into the Dupont Circle neighborhood. Enough effectively placed sculptures could provide a unique art walk that would also help orient visitors. The pedestals of the sculpture could have QR codes providing further information and help visitors to navigate the neighborhood, as well as reinforce historic and cultural information already provided on the kiosks.

Dupont Circle has always been an important cultural and historic neighborhood, and it is filled with many important cultural resources, such as The Phillips Collection, The DuPont Underground, and a number of art galleries and related art resources. It also has a significant number of important cultural resources and historic sites that are of interest to visitors. The neighborhood additionally has a number of important

All figures are courtesy of Brett Marden.

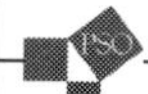

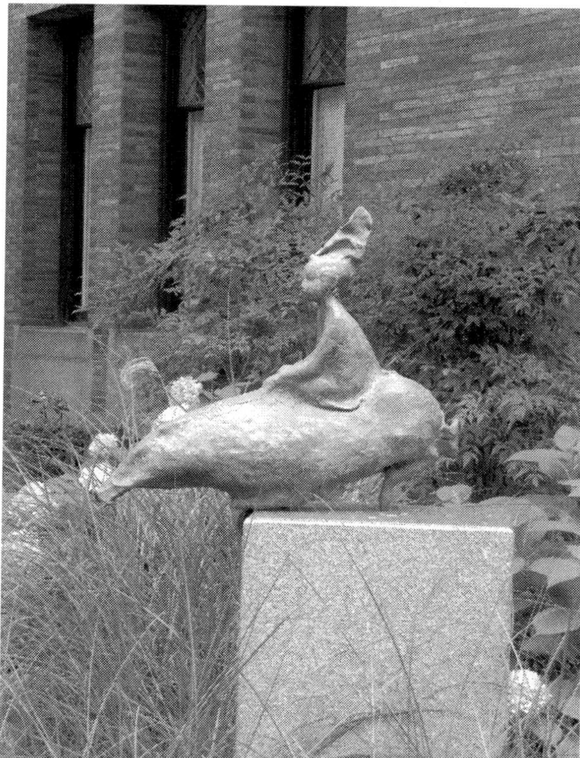

FIGURE 1 The sculpture *The Trip* by John Cavanaugh is instilled on the newly crated Cavanaugh Sculpture Park in DuPont Circle on the grounds of the Women's National Democratic Club Headquarters. It is a sculpture of a young girl astride a running boar and represents childhood in the park's theme of representing the four ages of women's life. It was Cavanaugh's first really successful sculpture that seemed to capture the sense of motion he was striving to discover in his work.

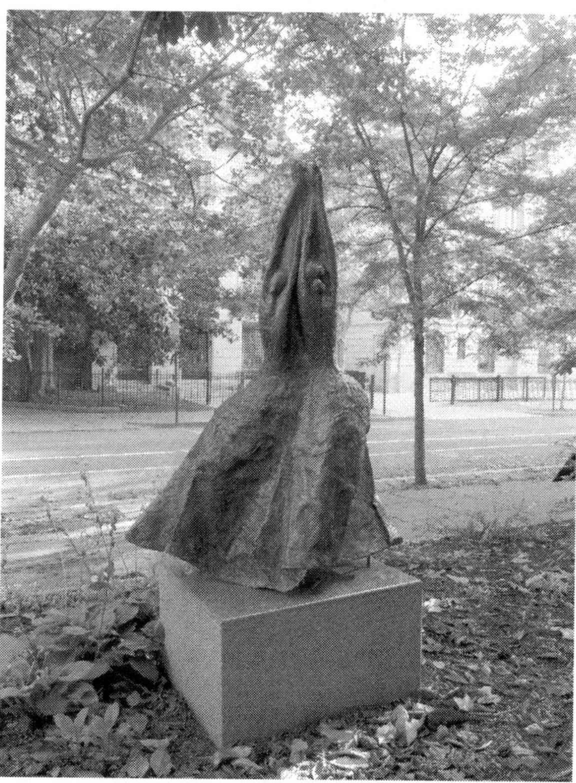

FIGURE 3 *Pas de Trois* is a life-sized sculpture of three young ballet dancers coming together with their hands held high and clasping each other. Installed on the grounds of the Cavanaugh Sculpture Park the sculpture represents adolescence in the four stages of women's lives, which is the theme of the park.

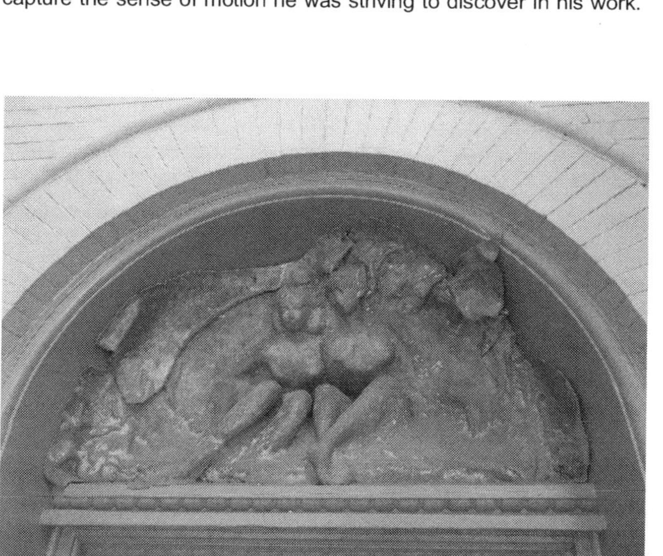

FIGURE 2 *Tympanum*, which is a sculpture that is placed above the front door of 1742 Corcoran Street NW in DuPont Circle, is a hammered relief sculpture of two young women reaching out above the entranceway. This is at Cavanaugh's residence building that he and Philip Froeder restored in 1969 and became his residence in Washington, DC.

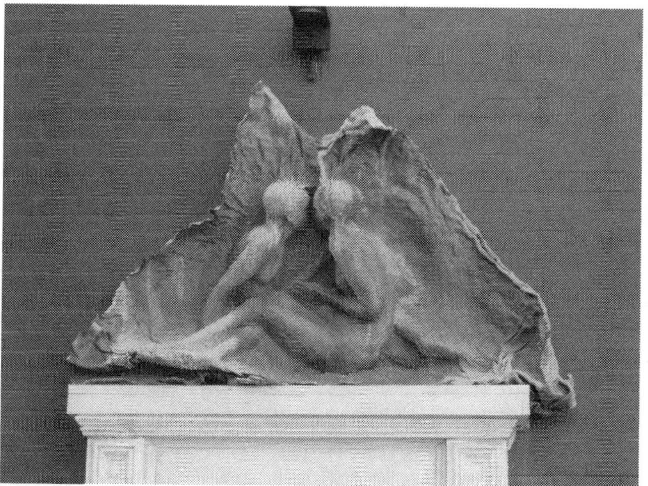

FIGURE 4 *Planting*, is a hammered lead relief of two girls appearing to emerge from a large seedpod, "almost kissing." This is based on a theme Cavanaugh developed for the seven relief sculptures he placed on the two restored 1880s houses he joined in 1978 in DuPont Circle. The building address, 1801–1803 Swann Street, used the themes of Proust's novel "Swann's Way" to influence the seven reliefs he placed on the buildings.

national headquarters and cultural and social institutions, as well as a large number of embassies that offer a great interest and appeal to tourists (Figure 5).

Central to the implementation of the Cavanaugh Walk, along with the John Cavanaugh Foundation and the Public Studies Organization, is the Dupont Circle Main Street Program. The director and members of the board have been actively involved in its success, as well as the Resilience Studio, which has been instrumental in graphically recording and providing drawings for The Walk.

Cavanaugh's sculpture in the Dupont Circle area is not the only reason Cavanaugh is important to the neighborhood, as he was also actively involved with its recovery from serious urban decline. He and his partner, architect and urban planner Philip Froeder, who moved to Washington in the 1960s, were directly involved in buying endangered properties and completely finishing projects that were crucial in the rehabilitation of Dupont Circle, which had fallen into blight and serious urban decay. In 1978, *The Washington Star* published their weekend magazine, which featured on the cover the work of Cavanaugh and Froeder. It focused on what they were doing to help rebuild the Dupont Circle Area. Titled *The Preservationists of DC*, the article featured in detail the outstanding work the two were doing to push back the critical urban blight that had taken over Dupont Circle. The in-depth piece pointed out that after the Dupont Circle neighborhood had been redlined—a term used to denote that banks and lending institutions would not provide loans to the area, that a handful of individuals, including Cavanaugh and Froeder had used their own resources and funds to recover and restore critical infrastructure to help restore the neighborhood.

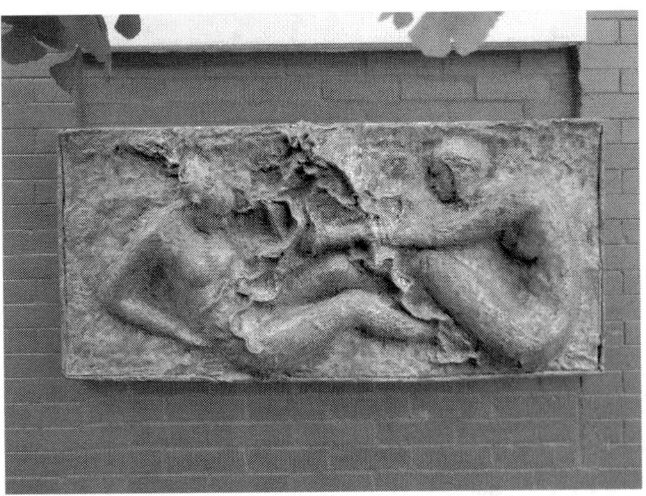

FIGURE 5 *Rooting*, "Represents a Budding Grove in the form of a planter encasing two girls in roots … entwined around them … The Rooting." "My notion here is sometimes a kiss can root deeply within you, perhaps more deeply than it should." J. C.

This well-documented and positive article also noted in depth the advanced improvements they had featured in upgrading the building in an effort to encourage young professionals and artists to move back into the DuPont Circle neighborhood. The article illustrated the importance of the new modern bathrooms and kitchens that had been installed in the apartments, as well as the freestanding fireplaces with historic tiles incorporated in the design and other modern features that would be crucial in attracting young renters.

The magazine also highlighted the seven unique hammered lead relief sculptures that Cavanaugh had installed on the façade of the building. These sculptures were inspired by the seven themes from Prost's book *Swann's Way*. A friend, who also had contributed to their projects, Doctor Albert Latucha, thought that the Swann connection could elicit an unusual artistic appreciation and connection to the site.

The Swann Street project was just one of a number of projects that Cavanaugh and Froeder had purchased and restored in a similar manner. Beginning in the late 1960s, they had successfully restored a number of apartment buildings and either sold these or kept them as income-producing rental sites. This included the 1742 Corcoran building, which became their home and which also included three rental apartments. On a number of these restorations, Cavanaugh created extraordinarily brilliant and unique hammered lead reliefs that were placed on the façade of the buildings.

To understand the role Cavanaugh played in the art of the 20th century and appreciate how significant his sculpture is, it is possible to look at his work as it is organized in Maren Stange's section of the Cavanaugh catalog, *In Search of Motion*. In it she divided Cavanaugh's work into three periods; the Columbus, Ohio, the New York City, and the Washington, DC periods. And before examining these periods, it's important to understand how already advanced he was in his artistic abilities at an early age. When he was only 8, Cavanaugh's father had died, and his mother was left raising four boys on her own (Figure 6). Cavanaugh was seen early on as a gifted young artist. So, his mother, made a bold move, and without having any prior contacts, took Cavanaugh to see Alice Archer Sewell James, who was a well-known figure in the Ohio art world, as the leader of the well known Urbana Movement. Cavanaugh's mother asked her directly if she would be willing to accept Cavanaugh as a student, which was a surprisingly direct approach. Interestingly, she did accept Cavanaugh as a student after seeing the boy's work his mother had brought to the meeting (Figure 7).

And so, Cavanaugh's early life was to provide an unusual opportunity for him to advance. With this access to such an advanced level of education, he matured quickly as did his abilities as an artist. And

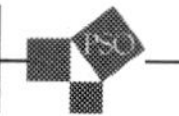

when he had completed the equivalent of his high school education, Mrs. James gave him some money and told him that he needed to go to the university, specifically to improve his English. Subsequently, he was able to attend Ohio State University on a special need's scholarship, and because of his extraordinary skills in art, largely due to his time spent with Mrs. James, he completed his undergraduate work in just 3 years. He then advanced to his graduate education where he specialized in ceramics and ceramic glazes. Here he had a great deal of success in producing brilliant works of ceramic sculpture, and also gave him an opportunity to become actively involved in the local art scene. A piece of his ceramic art was later incorporated into the permanent collection in the Columbus Museum of Art (Figure 8).

As a very active participant in several of the arts organizations, including becoming an officer in the Columbus Art League, he was very successful in his ceramic output, as well as in the significant sales of his artwork. He was also successful in several art exhibitions he entered and was awarded important prizes at the Emerson and Antioch exhibitions. He also received a Ford Foundation Grant at the Pennsylvania Academy of Arts Exhibition. One of his most prestigious awards came as an offer for a full scholarship and a one-person exhibition at the Cranbrook Academy of Art, which at the time was one of the top two graduate schools in the United States. However, he could not accept the full offer because he was just starting a young family,

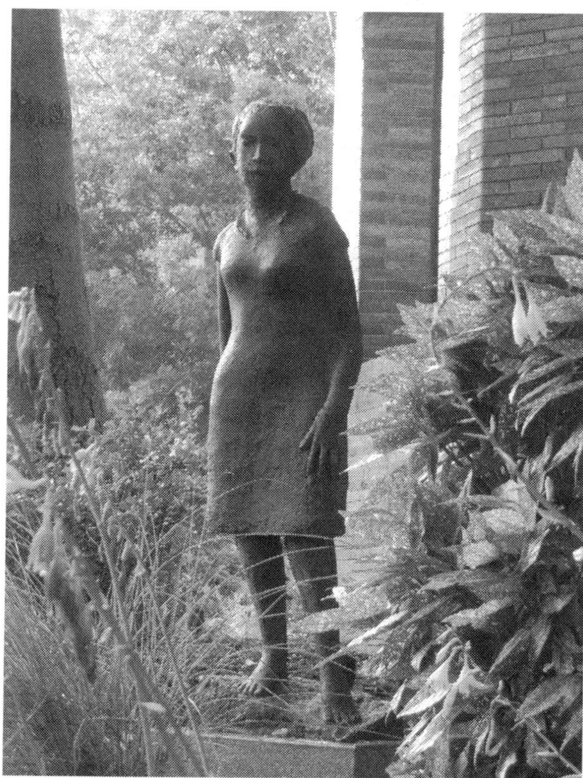

FIGURE 6 *Standing Female* is a sculpture of an older woman, that represents the final stage of a woman's life. The figure represented in this sculpture is said to suggest earlier photographs depicting Cavanaugh's mother.

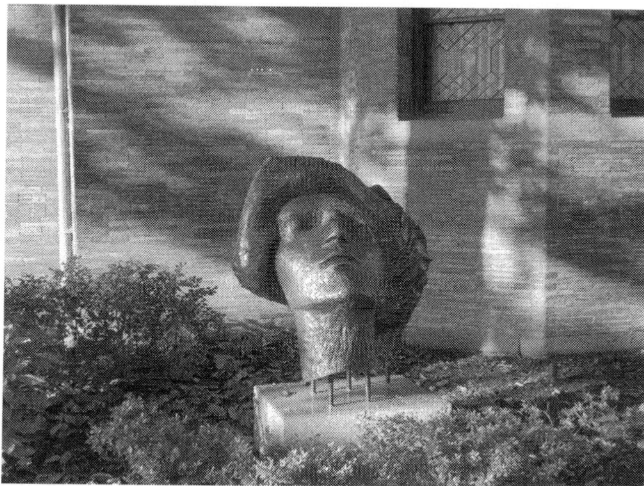

FIGURE 7 The sculpture of a Colossal head titled *Alice*. This image is said to be of Alice B. Toklas, who Cavanaugh admired. This is the third sculpture in the series in the Cavanaugh Sculpture Garden and represents middle age in the four stages of a woman's life.

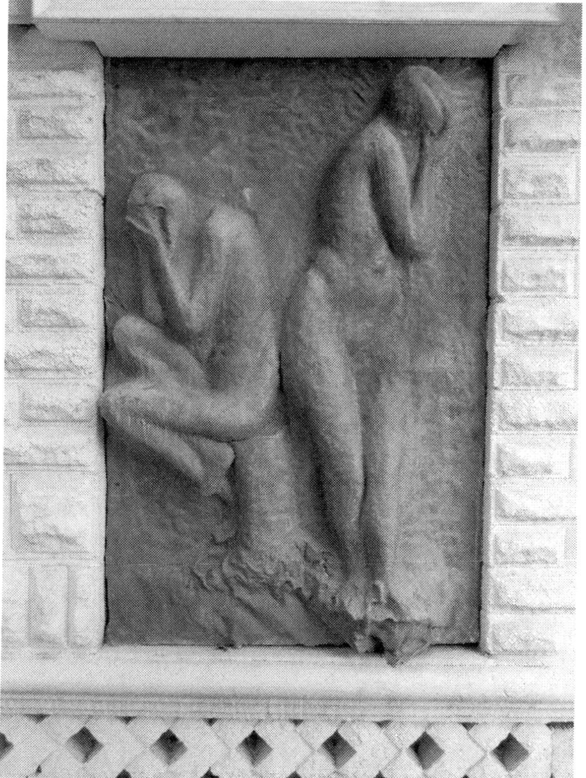

FIGURE 8 *Thorning*, the image of two young girls entangled in thorns. Cavanaugh felt it "...symbolizes The Prisoner, represented by two women caught in thorns. The intimation is that after the delight of flower picking, you find that everything in life is not kind."

however, he was able to accept the one-person exhibit at the prestigious school's galleries. In 1957, distracted and emotionally distraught, he left everything, including his family, and he abruptly left for New York City with only a trench coat and a toothbrush in his pocket (Figure 9).

His trip to New York resulted from a crisis, but it allowed him to enter a new life. Fortunately, he was eventually able to secure a position at the Sculpture Center in Manhattan. Since he was able to manage all of the kilns at the Center because of his background and training, he was given studio space at the center, and he was also able to participate in the Center's important exhibitions.

Cavanaugh was very successful in New York City, often receiving positive critical reviews from several media, even from The New York Times and the Herald Tribune for his work. As he continued to advance, he began to successfully complete work in hammered lead, which was difficult for most other sculptors (Figure 10). This success allowed him to immediately have a marketable sculpture, as well as develop a unique skill set that attracted public interest and publicity. He continued to have numerous sales and developed important contacts and clients in New York. He was also able to bring his work in hammered lead to a very high level. This was quite valuable, as other talented sculptors who tried to create works in lead were unable to reach the skill level Cavanaugh had achieved, and could only complete low relief lead sculpture, if at all, whereas Cavanaugh could even achieve life sized works in the round. In a much later solo exhibitions in 1996 in New York City, at the galleries of the National Sculpture Society, *The American Artist* magazine in their review of his exhibit, declared him "the Master of Hammered Lead." After a time in New York City in 1963, he decided that for a more affordable workspace necessary to sculpt and for a much calmer lifestyle, he would move to Washington, DC.

Cavanaugh's output increased significantly after he established his studio in Washington, and he continued to create sculpture in ceramic, bronze, and lead. Several of his exhibitions at the Sculpture Center in Manhattan, which continued theough 1970's, and his annual exhibits in Washington, DC, were very successful; some were almost completely sold out. In the mid-70s until his illness in 1983, he turned most of his attention to his hammered lead sculpture. His major sculptures and focus were his study of dancers that he

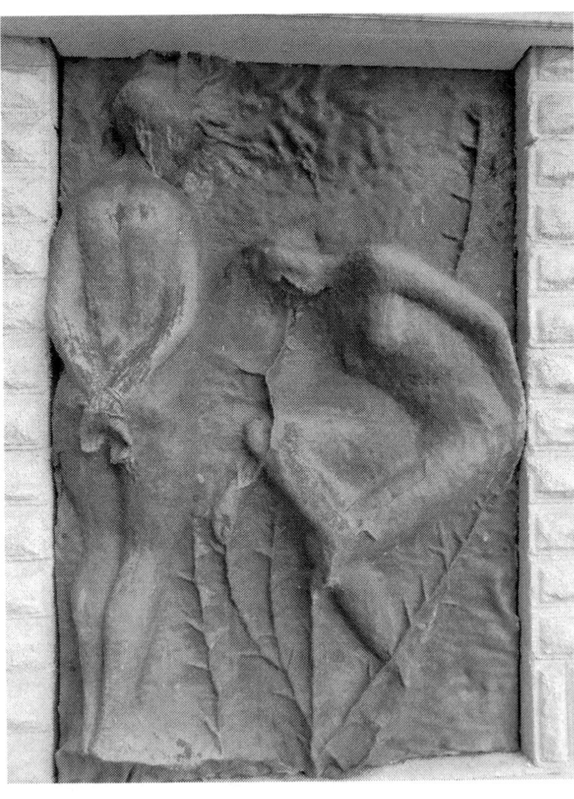

FIGURE 9 *Sodom and Gomorrah*, is a hammered lead relief panel that is adjacent to *Thorning*, and is a companion panel to it. It depicts two girls standing together bound by their hands. Cavanaugh wrote "...as represented by pruning. The idea is that after thorning, if you get rid of all the ideas you can't lie with, strong root will prevail."

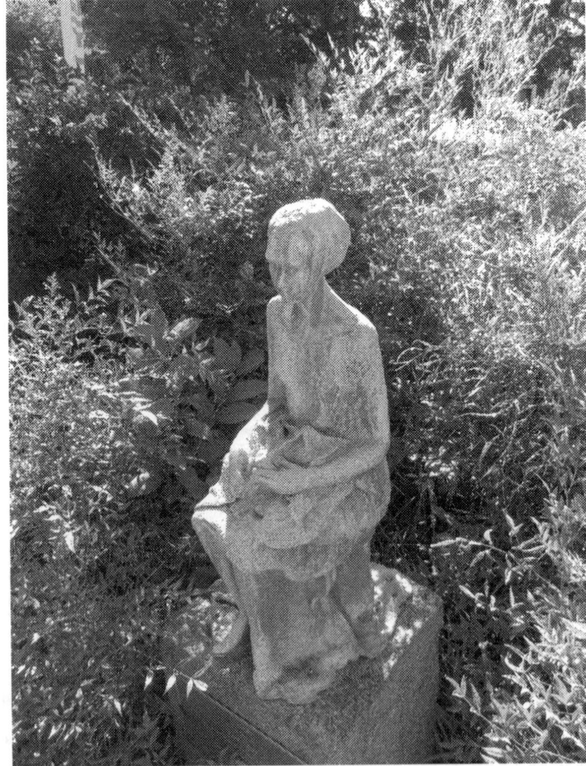

FIGURE 10 Sculpture of *Demeter*, goddess of agriculture, which is a hammered lead sculpture installed in the gardens of the National Arboretum in Washington, DC. It is the only figurative sculpture on the grounds and was installed to honor Kya Lahr, who was responsible for organizing and implementing the volunteer service for The National Arboretum.

pursued after his attendance at the Kennedy Center in Washington, and through backstage studies he was able to make, which influenced the direction he took in his work. He successfully completed several life-sized sculptures of dancers and other robed figures, which represented his most idealistic work. Several of these were purchased and installed in public settings in Colorado, Ohio, and Connecticut. The Marriott Hotel chain purchased a number of his dancers and installed them in their gardens and entry foyers, including hotel settings in California, North Carolina, Virginia, and Maryland. His last full exhibition that he finished before his death in January of 1985, was a unique installation of 21 topiary figures he created for the National Arboretum Greenhouse on Capitol Hill next to the US Capitol building. These were exceptional hammered lead sculptures of birds and animals that he paired with plants selected by the Arboretum staff that uniquely matched each sculpture (Figure 11).

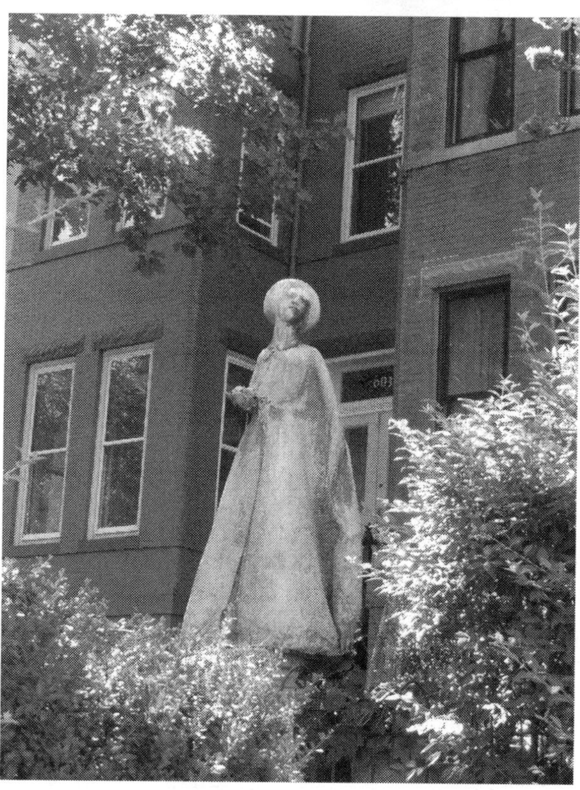

FIGURE 11 Life-sized sculpture of *Olive Risley Seward*, which was placed adjacent to Seward Square in Northeast Washington, DC. The Sculpture represents the daughter of Secretary of the Interior, William Seward who was known for his connection with the purchase of Alaska from Russia. The sculpture was created in the basement of a building adjacent to the square that Cavanaugh and Froeder were restoring and later installed in the front yard adjacent to the Square.

Besides his success with his new sculpture activities, he remained actively involved in the Dupont Circle neighborhood affairs. After his death, organized neighborhood historic walks would often highlight his sculpture. Even earlier, the Smithsonian Associates Program occasionally organized neighborhood historic walks in Dupont Circle that would include Cavanaugh's sculpture, as Cavanaugh had led a number of Smithsonian sculpture classes demonstrating the creation of hammered lead sculpture. One of the popular national travel guides also featured his reliefs in the Washington, DC, section in one of their published guides calling attention to the unique role Cavanaugh art played in Dupont Circle.

The Cavanaugh Walk is a totally unique public art event. The idea of an expansion is unusual as it is exciting. And there is not another art project focusing on a single sculptor's work like it on such a scale in any major city—anywhere. Besides the unique aesthetic value and experience, the Walk provides a clever visual draw that engages the visiting public to experience something new and exciting. Visually it is as powerful as it is enlightening.

DOI: 10.1002/smo3.12005

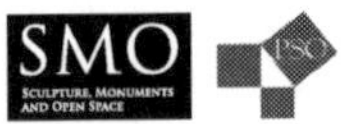

ARTICLE

Inside out is in: Pritzker Prize Laureate 2024—Riken Yamamoto

B. D. Kerrick

Washington DC, USA

Correspondence
B. D. Kerrick, Freelance Writer and Journalist specializing in the Arts, Washington DC, USA.
Email: writereditor@duck.com

The text is a brief biography and philosophical observation of the subject's approach to his craft, whereas the images and captions consider his and other relevant works concretely. Most of the images are shown in chronological order of the subject's creation and most of the figure number references in the text are arbitrary.

The Pritzker Architecture Prize, widely regarded as the Nobel Prize of Architecture, has tapped Riken Yamamoto to be the laureate for 2024 (Figure 1). As we go to press, Mr. Yamamoto is giving the Laureate Lecture, titled *Community: The Architect as a Catalyst for Change* at the College of Architects of the Illinois Institute of Technology. The lecture title is an apt motto for the architect whose career has embraced the theme of building community with buildings and encouraging edification through the edifice.

As a boy Riken Yamamoto often sat between his mother's pharmacy in the front of their house and the living quarters in the back, between two thresholds, as he thought of it. Born in 1945 in Beijing, PRC, he and his family relocated to their home country in Yokohama, Japan when he was four years old (Figures 2 and 3).

His childhood threshold experience prepared him for an epiphany he had as a young college graduate visiting traditional villages across the world. His group of travel companions included his professor, Hiroshi Hara, who was to become an eminent architect in his own right (e.g., Kyōto Station, Umeda Sky Building, Yamato International, Sapporo Dome) (Figures 4 and 5).

From the Mediterranean countries to the Americas to the Middle East to the Indian subcontinent, Riken Yamamoto discovered a widespread theme in which traditional village homes conjoined public and private spaces, just as did the typical Japanese townhouse known as a Machiya in Yokohama, Japan, in which he grew up. Of these various village structures it was the Greek oikos housing and its innate inducement to

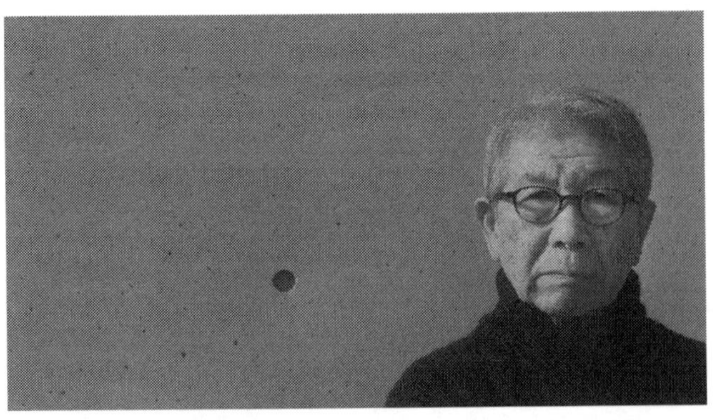

FIGURE 1 Riken Yamamoto. Photo courtesy of Tom Welsh and Pritzker Prize.

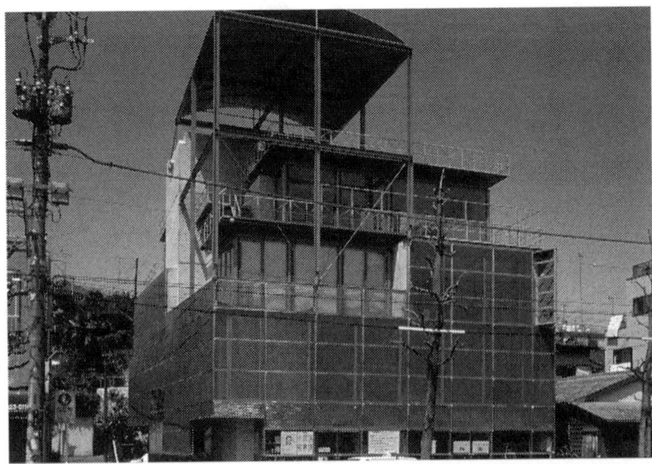

FIGURE 2 Gazebo, 1986, Yokohama, Japan. This is the house Riken Yamamoto designed as his own residence. Photo courtesy of Ryuji Miyamoto and Pritzker Prize.

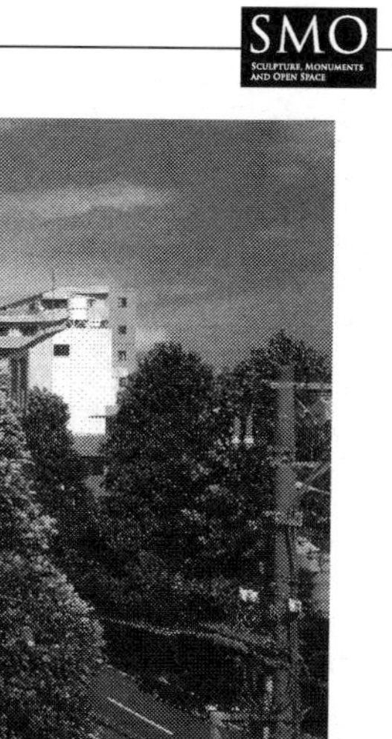

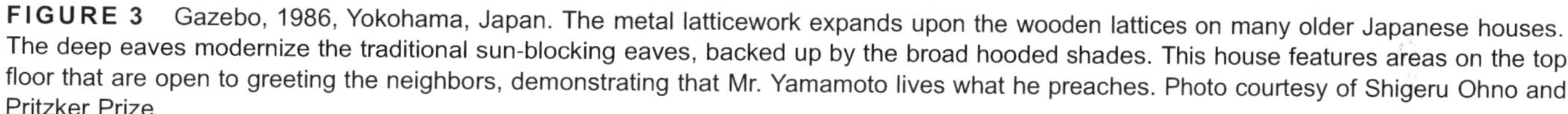

FIGURE 3 Gazebo, 1986, Yokohama, Japan. The metal latticework expands upon the wooden lattices on many older Japanese houses. The deep eaves modernize the traditional sun-blocking eaves, backed up by the broad hooded shades. This house features areas on the top floor that are open to greeting the neighbors, demonstrating that Mr. Yamamoto lives what he preaches. Photo courtesy of Shigeru Ohno and Pritzker Prize.

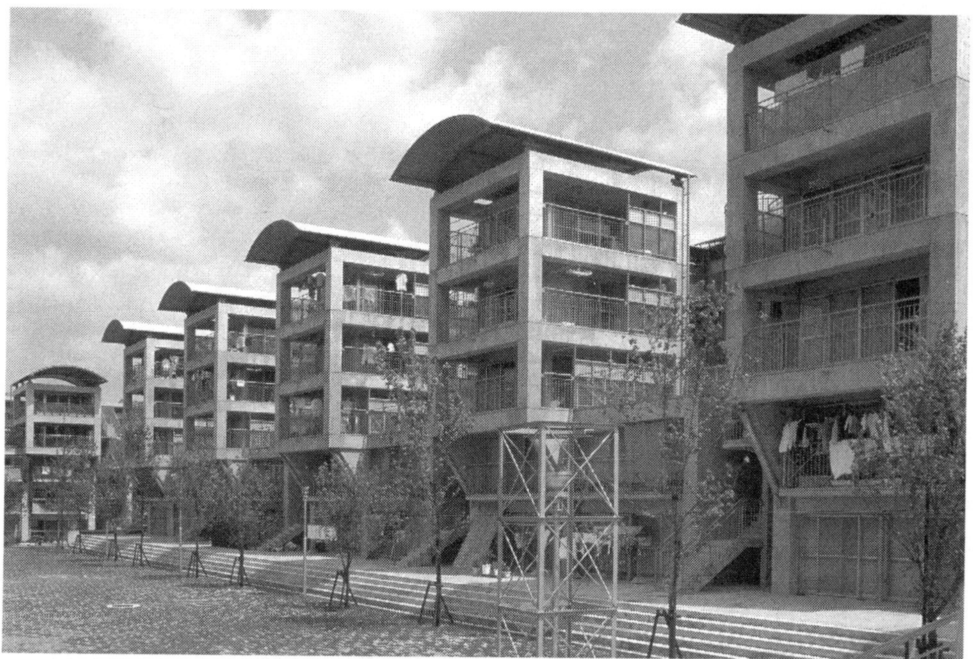

FIGURE 4 Hotakubo Housing,1991, Kumamoto, Japan. The metal latticework and hooded sun shade are explored again in this social housing project. Likewise, community is encouraged by open terraces facing a square enclosed by the units. Photo courtesy of Tomio Ohashi and Pritzker Prize.

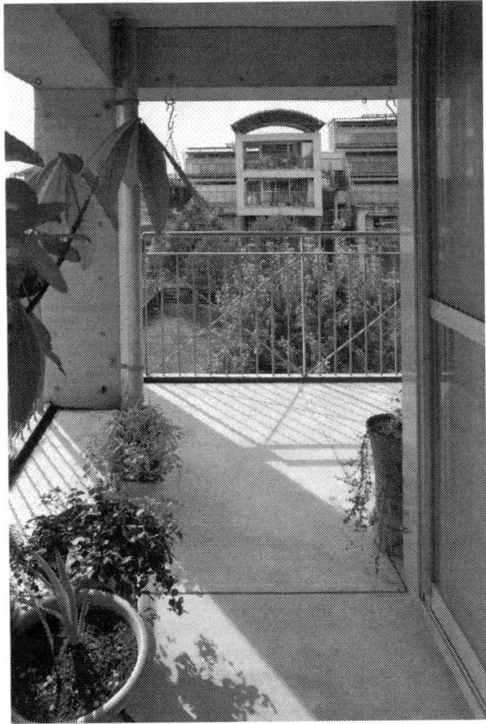

FIGURE 5 Hotakubo Housing, 1991, Kumamoto, Japan. Photo courtesy of Tomio Ohashi and Pritzker Prize.

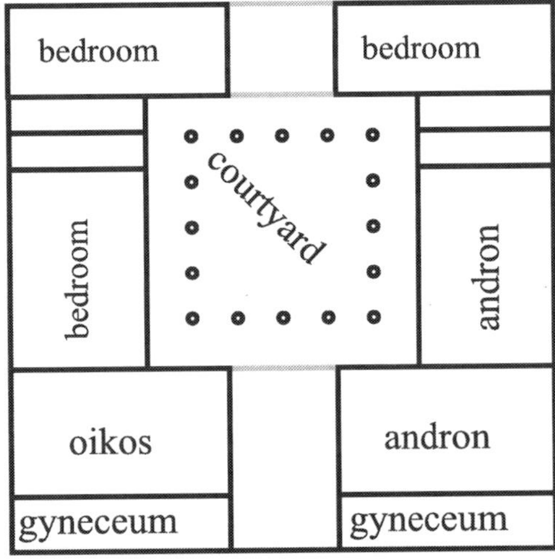

FIGURE 6 The oikoi in ancient Greece influenced the young architect student in his worldwide travels during his stopover in Greece. An Oikos was a Greek house with a courtyard. The colonnaded courtyard was private from the community but communal to the family and servants. The andron was the men's room, the gyneceum was the women's room, and the word oikos was used for the family room, for the whole house, and even for the household comprising the family and their servants. Illustrator unnamed. License: Public Domain Mark (PDM).

community adhesion along with the machiya that influenced him the most (Figures 6 and 7).

But before college he had what he described as his "first experience with architecture" as he looked up at the awe-inspiring five-story pagoda at the ancient Kôfuku-ji Temple, in Nara, Japan, illuminated only by the moon (Figure 8).

During his college years Mr. Yamamoto visited Osaka Expo '70 and was transfixed by the simplicity of the United States exhibit with its moon rock display, and observed that the architecture was little more than "air and the small stone" (Figures 9 and 10).

Another major influence upon his later works was one of his own earliest assignments, the 1977 Yamakawa Villa in Nagano, Japan. The work in turn appears to channel the Machiya of his childhood. The client provided only a handful of vague instructions for a summer house in the woods with which the unseasoned young architect formulated a brilliantly unique design. Several separate block-like rooms sit upon a deck with a single gable roof covering them all, but without common walls to contain all the rooms together (Figures 11 and 12).

> ***"For me, to recognize space, is to recognize an entire community."***

He has carried the openness and transparency of the individualistic Yamakawa Villa into the rest of his career, and many of Mr. Yamamoto's later projects continue to express his evolving philosophy on the responsibility of architects to encourage community. Riken Yamamoto himself best describes his design philosophy. He says, "For me, to recognize space, is to recognize an entire community." By way of elaboration he says, "The current architectural approach emphasizes privacy, negating the necessity of societal relationships (Figure 13). However, we can still honor the freedom of each individual while living together in architectural space as a republic, fostering harmony across cultures and phases of life."

He has said that the writings of Hannah Arendt have inspired him. The philosopher did indeed explore the universal importance of the golden rule of neighborliness in her early essay *Love and Saint Augustine*, and the theme permeates her later writings (Figure 14).

And so it is that the influences upon Mr. Yamamoto, whether they be the pagoda, the machiya, the oikos, or books and essays, are not so much directly evident in his designs as philosophically evident. Generally, his approach to architecture calls to mind the "responsive communitarianism" that was evolving in the late 20th Century and coalesced into the named movement in the 1990s and which encouraged a balance between individual rights and social responsibilities and engagement (Figure 15).

Indeed, Mr. Yamamoto *encourages* social cohesion. As the Pritzker Prize's jury citation says, Mr. Yamamoto "suggests rather than imposes this shared dimension

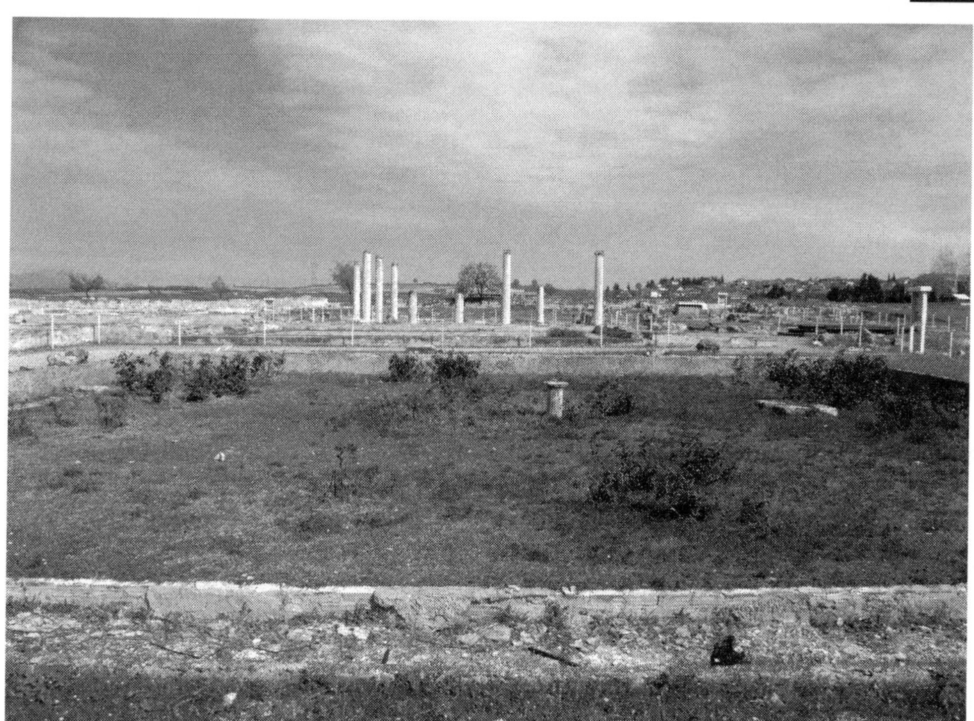

FIGURE 7 The House of Dionysos, 235-300 BCE, Pella, Central Macedonia, Greece. This ancient private house, or oikos, was graced by a large courtyard encircled by a grand peristyle and another, smaller peristyle courtyard. Photo by Carole Raddato from FRANKFURT, Germany. CC-BY-SA 2.0.

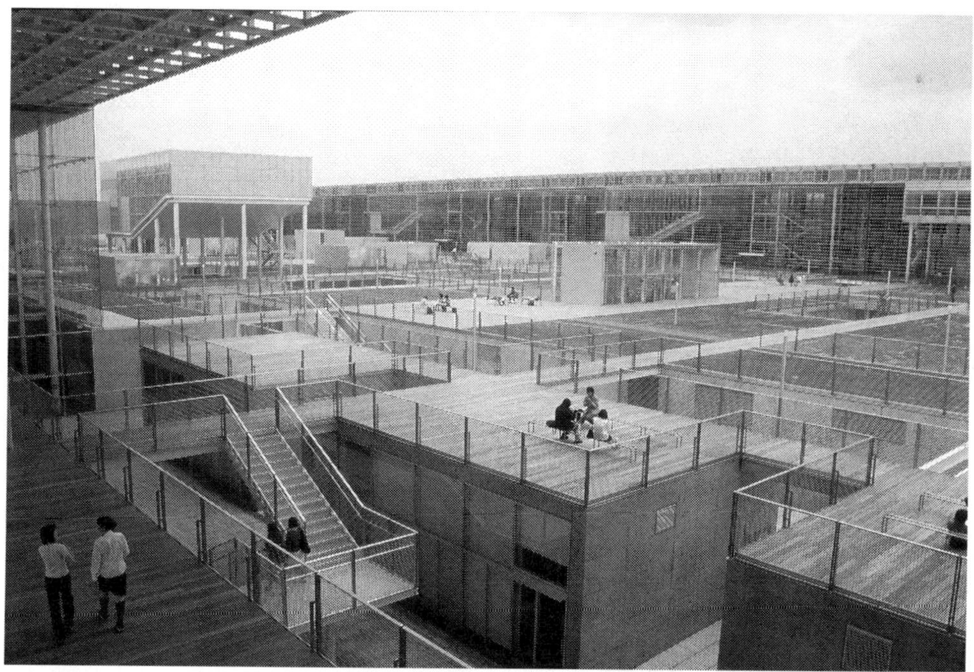

FIGURE 8 Saitama Prefectural University, 1991, Koshigaya, Japan. Demonstrating the architect's priorities of social connection and interdisciplinary continuity, the vagueness of the boundaries among the various buildings in a mysterious way aesthetically cohere the classrooms, auditorium, library, faculty rooms, administrative offices, gymnasium, and cafeteria. Photo courtesy of Riken Yamamoto, Field Shop and Pritzker Prize.

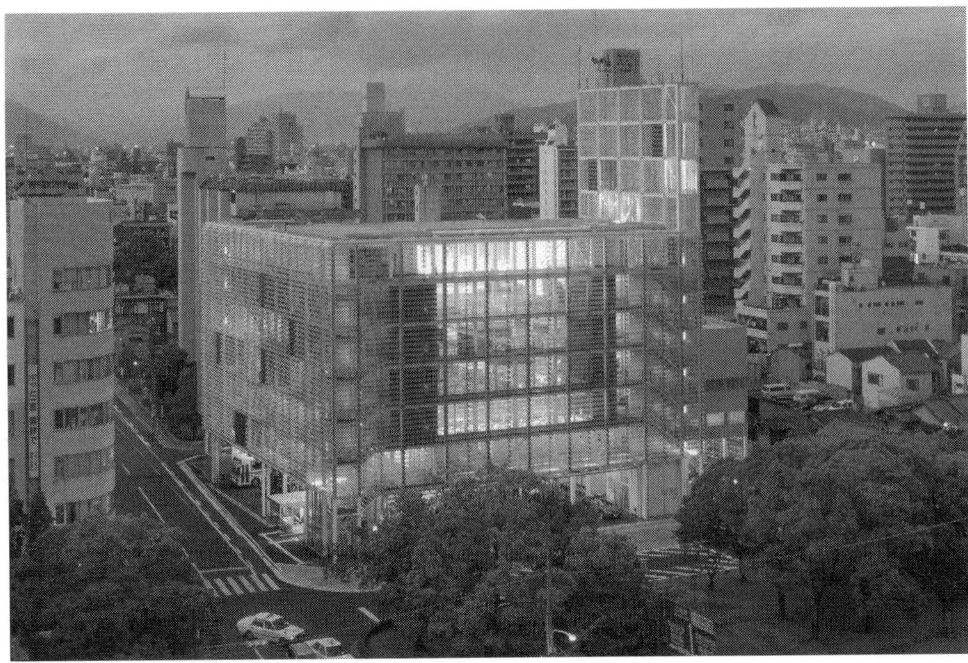

FIGURE 9 Hiroshima Nishi Fire Station, 2000, Hiroshima, Japan. The transparency of the fire station intends a philosophical approach that happens to invert the purpose of Jeremy Bentham's hypothetical panopticon prison. The late 18th century panopticon theoretically allows unobservable authorities from a deck within to observe the subjects, the prisoners, and passageways in multiple floors of cells surrounding the deck, whereas the transparent outer and many inner walls of the fire station invites free citizens to watch at anytime an entity of their government in action, specifically, firefighters training and preparing for emergencies. Photo courtesy of Tomio Ohashi and Pritzker Prize.

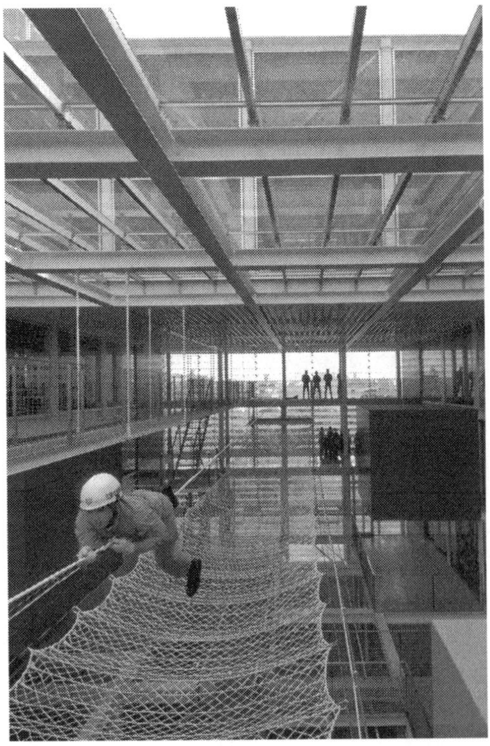

FIGURE 10 Hiroshima Nishi Fire Station, 2000, Hiroshima, Japan. Photo courtesy of Tomio Ohashi and Pritzker Prize.

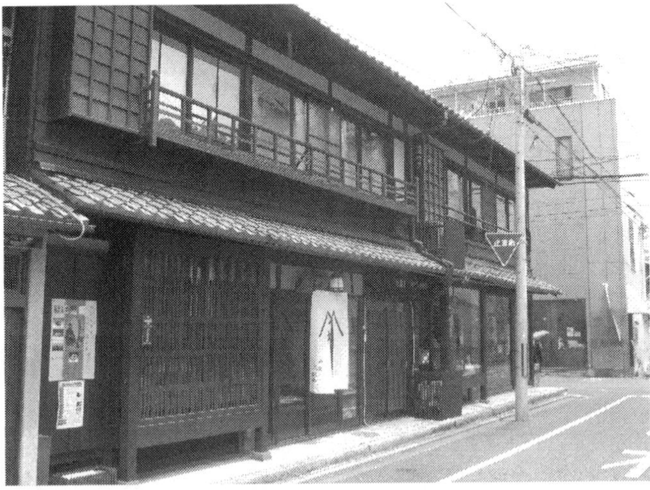

FIGURE 11 The Machiya, or traditional Japanese townhouse, as illustrated by this example, was the type of house in which the future architect grew up and which imparted a lasting influence upon him. The machiya typically contains within its outer walls one or two gardens to let in space and air and to provide tranquility. The eaves are often deep to shield the house from the hot summer sun. Preceding the last few decades of modernization in Japanese cities, the close placement of machiya between narrow streets and, often, alleyways, strongly enhanced community bonding. "Yamasada." Photo by Mariemon, Permission: GFDL, CC-BY-3.0.

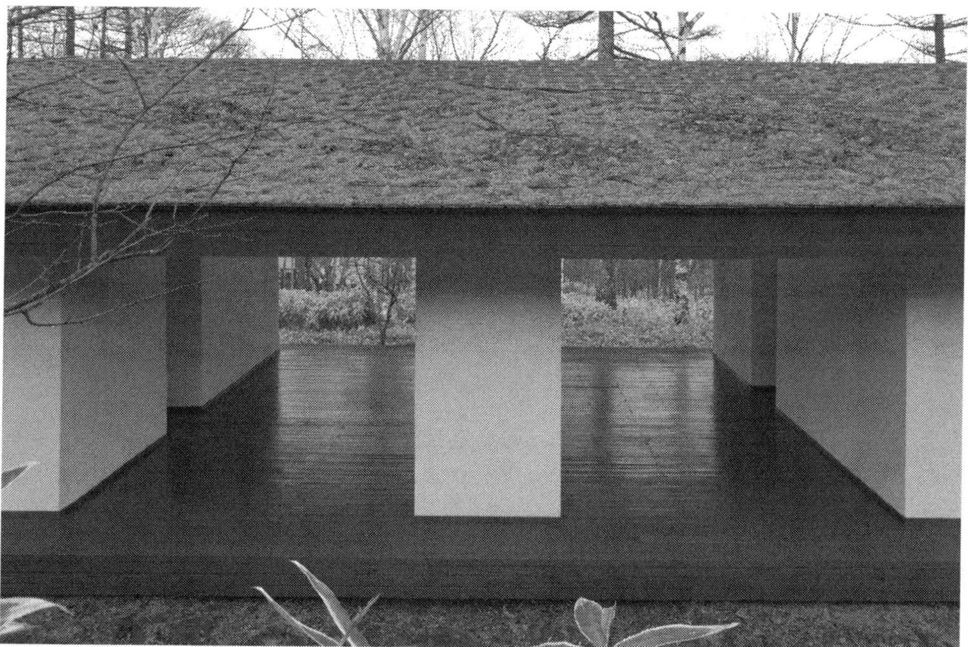

FIGURE 12 Yamakawa Villa, 1977, Yatsugatake, Japan. Designed in the beginning of Mr. Yamamoto's career, this private summer house in wooded country bears some resemblance to the summer setup of certain traditional houses in Kyoto. In those houses, translucent sliding doors called shoji could be opened wide to allow air to circulate. This revealed the rooms to the street and, incidentally, visually separated the rooms. Yamakawa Villa is unique in that the rooms are truly separated by outdoor spaces. Photo courtesy of Tomio Ohashi and Pritzker Prize.

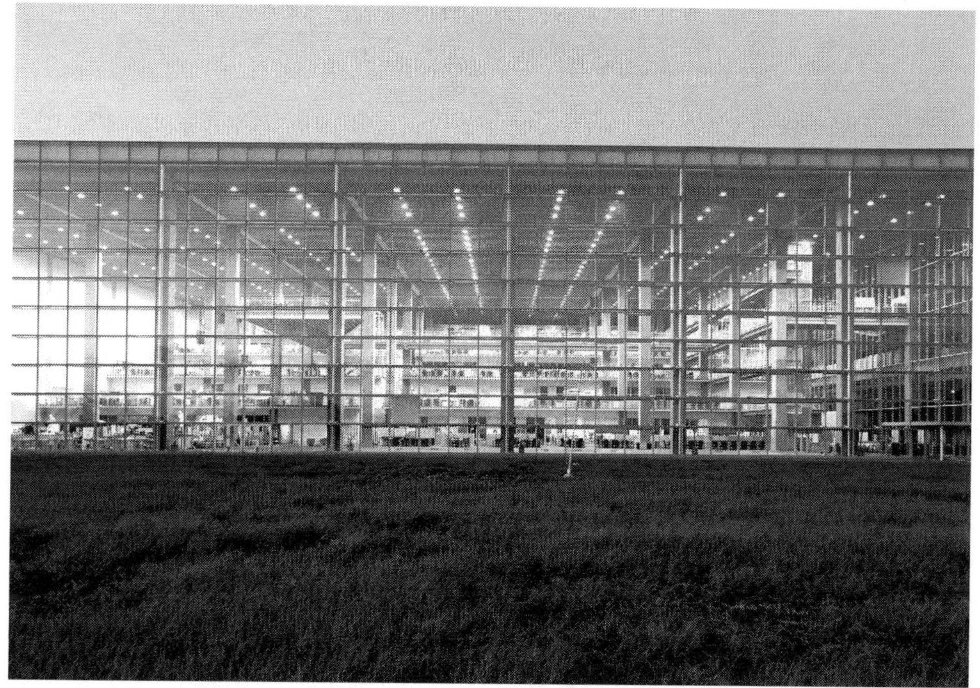

FIGURE 13 Future University of Hakodate, 2000, Hakodate, Japan. Taking cues from the fire station and SPU above, the university features transparent exterior and interior walls to promote a feeling of accessibility and connectedness between departments, classrooms, faculty research rooms, and between the university and the surrounding community. Photo courtesy of Isao Aihara and Pritzker Prize.

through understated, yet precise architectural interventions" (Figures 16 and 17).

Mr. Yamamoto has received many prestigious accolades in addition to the Pritzker Prize, including appointment as Academician by the International Academy of Architecture, the Japan Institute of Architects Award, the Public Buildings Prize (twice), the Good Design Gold Award (twice), the Prize of

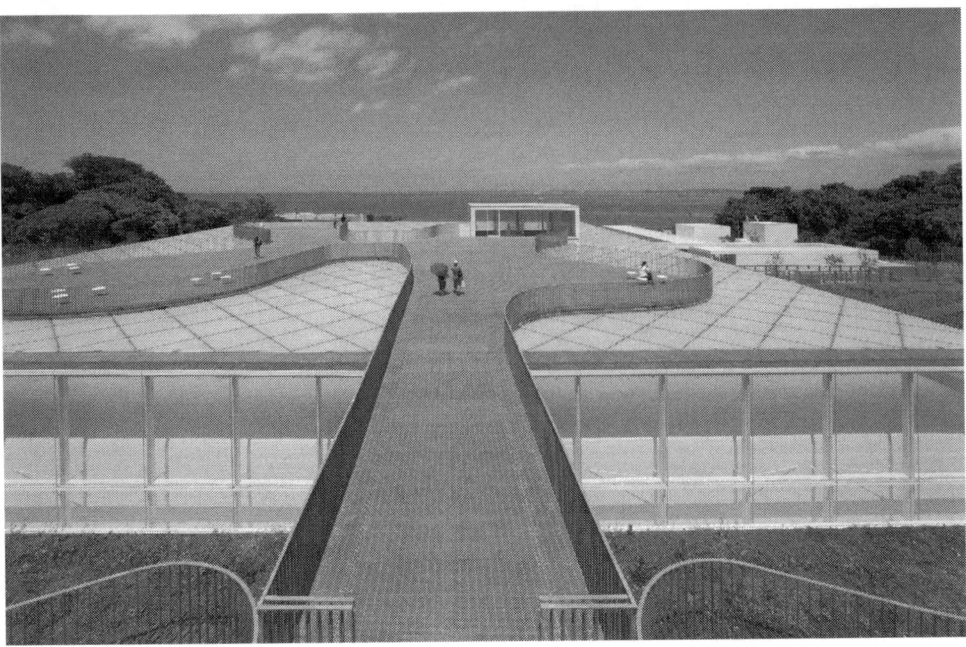

FIGURE 14 Yokosuka Museum of Art, 2007 Yokosuka, Japan. The architect again uses his favorite materials glass and metal to create a sense of unity among visitors and between visitors and the environment. A massive perambulatory path, evoking the reverential grounds about a Buddhist stupa, seems to float above a glassine-like surface that protects the artwork and its devotees below. Photo courtesy of Tomio Ohashi and Pritzker Prize.

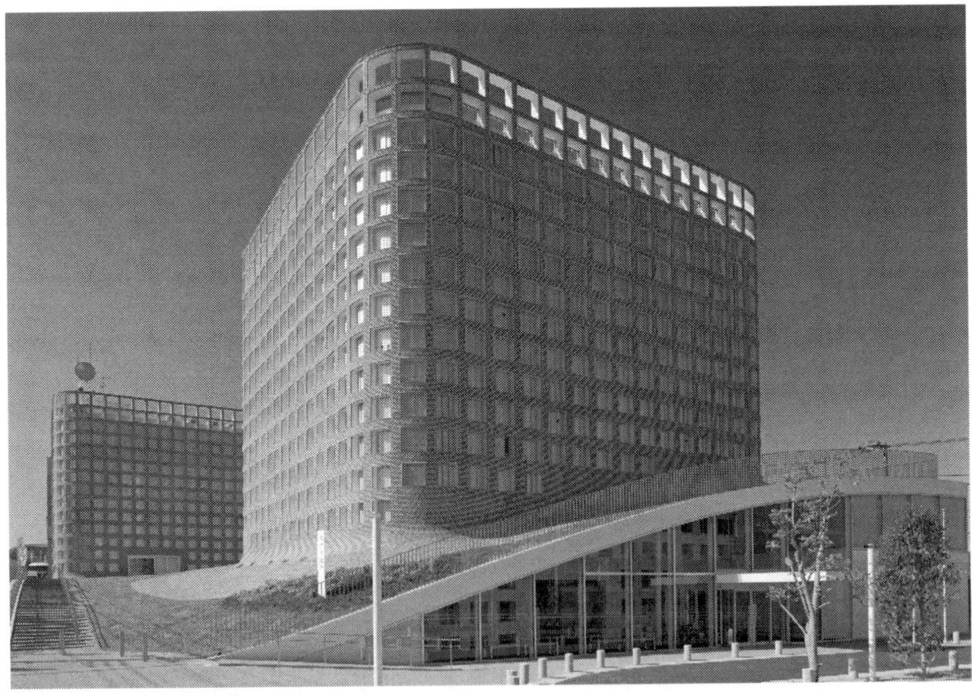

FIGURE 15 Fussa City Hall, 2008, Tokyo, Japan. A pair of relatively low-rising, earth tone civic buildings with cleanly punched out windows respectfully compliments the neighborhood. A man-made hilly concourse, which has become a popular space for public activities, rolls around the softly curved corners of the buildings and invites citizens to feel closer to their local government. Under the hollow hills are cavernous, Middle-Earth-like entrances that are walled in by glass and lead to spaces for additional public activities. Photo courtesy of Sergio Pirrone and Pritzker Prize.

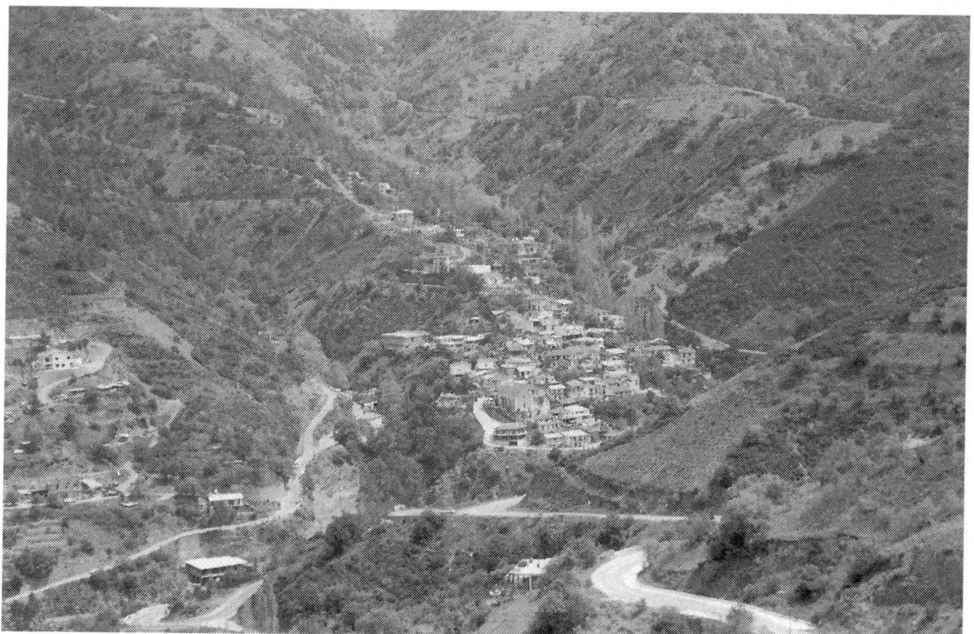

FIGURE 16 Modern day Oikos, Nicosia District, Republic of Cyprus, is a community of mostly boxy, sun-reflective houses nestled along a descending ridge between higher ridges. "Oikos, Troodos, Zypern." Photo by Bayreuth2009, Permission: GFDL, CC-BY-3.0.

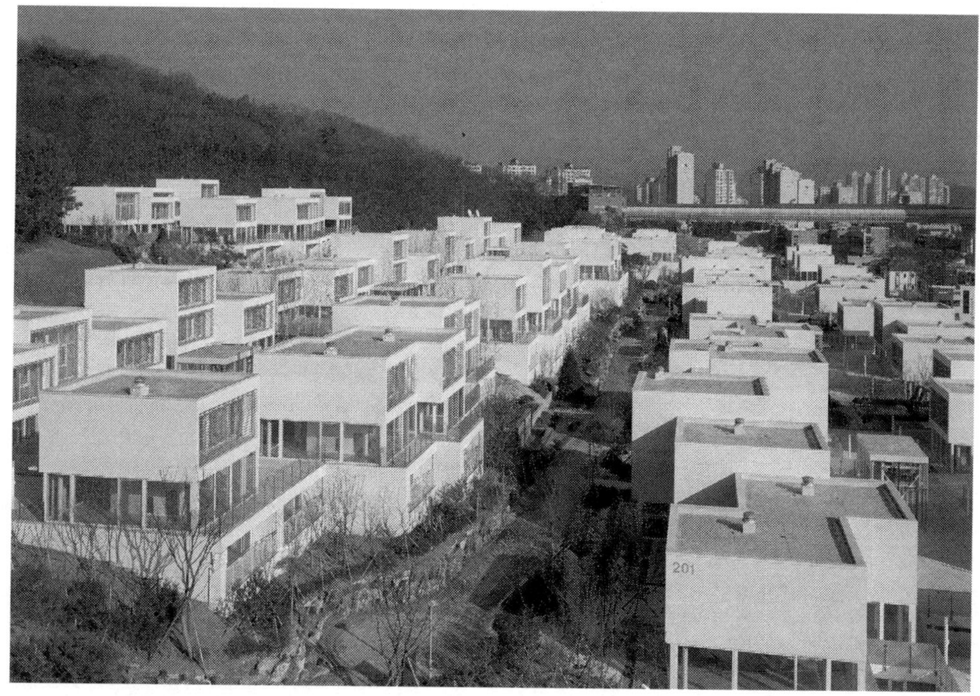

FIGURE 17 Pangyo Housing, Pangyo, Seongnam-si, Republic of Korea, designed in 2010 and completed in 2013. The complex of connected houses on a hillside bear a remarkable, modernized resemblance to present-day Oikos, Greece. The glass-walled, above-ground first floor of each house and the conjoined terraces within each section of houses provide opportunities for residents to interact. The nine sections of houses are further joined by bridges. The complex contains additional social spaces plus playgrounds and gardens. Photo courtesy of Kouichi Satake and Pritzker Prize.

the Architectural Institute of Japan (twice), the Japan Arts Academy Award, and the Mainichi Art Awards.

His landscape and building works are found across Japan, and in the Republic of Korea, the People's Republic of China, and Switzerland (Figures 18 and 19).

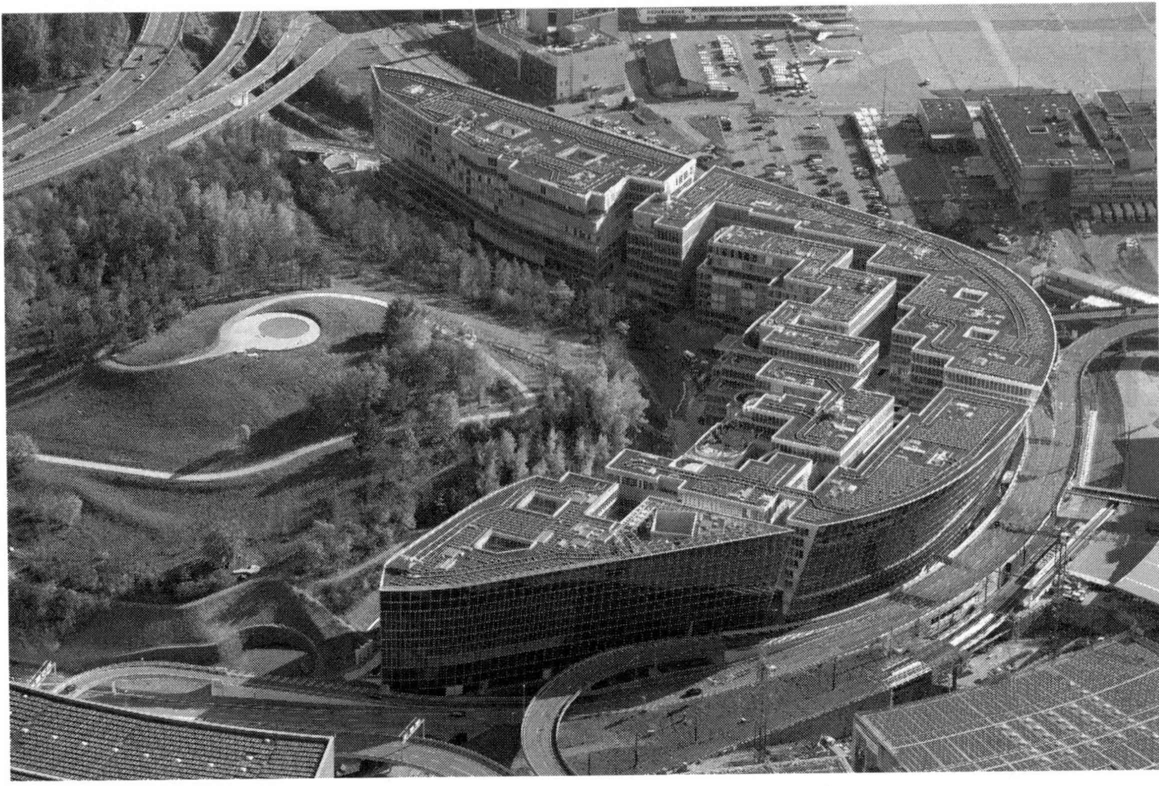

FIGURE 18 THE CIRCLE at Zürich Airport, 2020, Zürich, Switzerland. The complex of buildings are tied together by a ribbon of highway and the complex in turn gracefully embraces a park on a hill. The modernly curvaceous and gravity-defying walls on the convex side of the complex stand in sharp contrast to the boxy park-side. This boxy contour evokes the streetscape of the medieval Alstadt (old town) in Zürich. The shop-filled corridors within the complex conjure up the alleys cutting through the Münstergasse in the Alstadt. Mr. Yamamoto describes it as "not architecture but a city and an environment." Photo courtesy of Flughafen Zürich AG and Pritzker Prize.

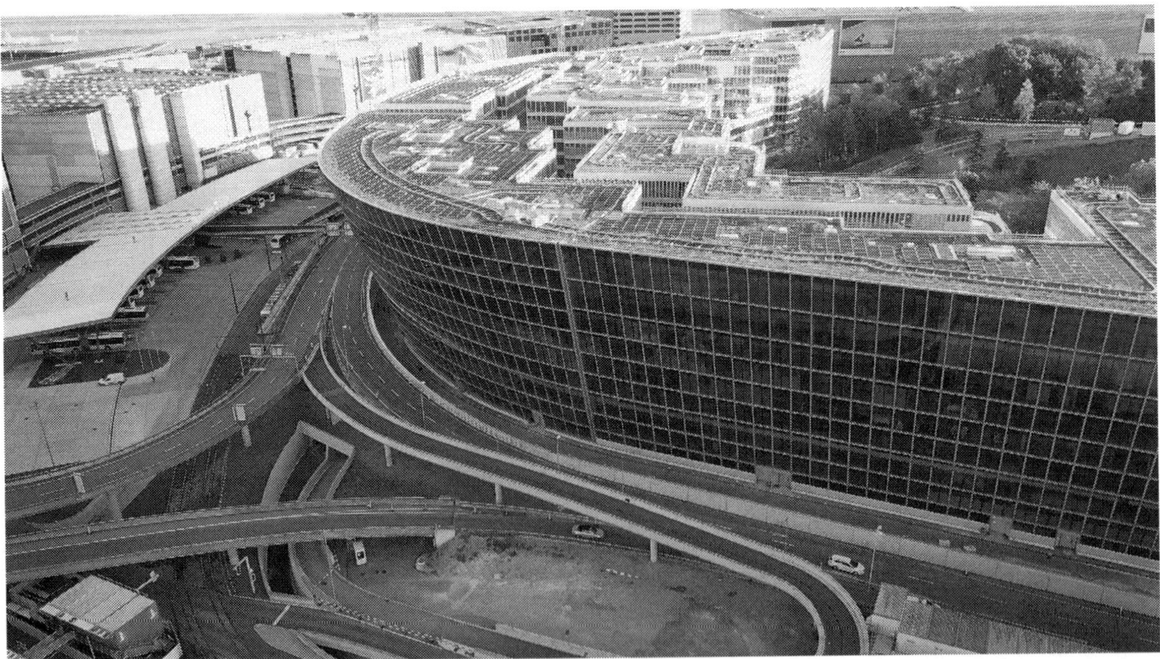

FIGURE 19 THE CIRCLE at Zürich Airport, The 2020, Zürich, Switzerland. Photo courtesy of Flughafen Zürich AG and Pritzker Prize.

Received: 19 May 2024 | Accepted: 11 June 2024

DOI: 10.1002/smo3.12003

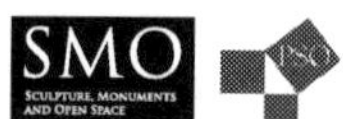

ARTICLE

Antonio Canova: The genius of Neoclassic sculpture

Rita Bartolo

Independent Writer, Arlington, VA, USA

Correspondence
Rita Bartolo, Independent Writer, Arlington, VA, USA.
Email: erita888@ymail.com

KEYWORDS
Antonio Canova; sculptor; artist; exhibition

Figures are courtesy of Brett Marden.

A uniquely curated and scholarly exhibition of the renowned Italian sculptor Antonio Canova opened last summer at the National Gallery of Art in Washington, DC, and closed this spring after a second venue at the Art Institute of Chicago. This exhibition titled *Canova: Sketches in Clay*, was remarkable in many ways and celebrates his many lesser-known but brilliant works in clay. Over 60 works are on display, including three dozen clay and terracotta sculptures that were included in the exhibition. There is little doubt that Canova was the most celebrated sculptor during the Neoclassic Period in art, which started in the late 18th century and reached its height in the early 19th century. Following the Rococo period of art in the 18th century, which featured a flamboyant and exaggerated style, the Neoclassic artists created a style that was inspired by idealism and the perfection of form that was significantly influenced by classical work of Greece and Rome, as well as inspired by the recent classic treasures that were being uncovered in the excavations in Pompeii. During this effort and the ongoing discovery of classical sculpture and art, many European artists traveled to Rome to have an opportunity to examine the unique finds that were being retrieved from a variety of excavations in Italy, which became the central inspiration to artists during the Neoclassical period. Canova also came to Rome and traveled through other historic parts of Italy while he was still in Venice to view these ancient treasures (Figure 1).

Eventually, Canova became the undisputed leader of the Neoclassical movement in sculpture, and along with Jacques Louis David in painting, they were admired and celebrated throughout Europe and Russia. Canova even completed a prominent marble sculpture of *George Washington*, which was installed in the state capital of North Carolina.

Canova's work was sought after by prominent collectors,members of the nobility and the political elite, that eventually included Napoleon and members of his family, who had gained a great deal of influence in European culture during the early 19th century. His collection included Canova's biographical marble, *Napoleon As Mars the Peacemaker*, as well as the study of his sister Pauline as *Venus Victrix* (Figure 2). Some of the most well-known neoclassical sculptures, such as *Psyche Revived by a Kiss*, *Daedalus and Icarus*, and *Theseus and the Minotaur*, are seen as clear examples that express neoclassic values and ideals (Figure 3). One of Canova's most recognized pieces, *The Three Graces* (Figures 4 and 5), was being completed for Princess Josephine, who had unfortunately died before it could be finished. A visiting client, the Duke of Bedford, saw the sculpture in Canova's studio in Rome and wanted to acquire it for his collection. However, Hector, Josephine's heir took possession of the sculpture and had it sent to Russia, where it is now being exhibited in the Hermitage Museum in Saint Petersburg. Canova then created a new version of *The Three Graces* for the Duke of Bedford, because of his enthusiasm for the work, which was then taken to England for his London estate. It is now in the collection of the Victoria And Albert Museum in London.

While many of us are familiar with a number of Canova's marble sculptures because of their popularity and importance, which we have seen in exhibitions or in museum collections, it has been over 50 years since Canova's clay and terracotta models have been included in an exhibition. The addition of his clay sketches, which were fired to preserve them, has shown us the skilled

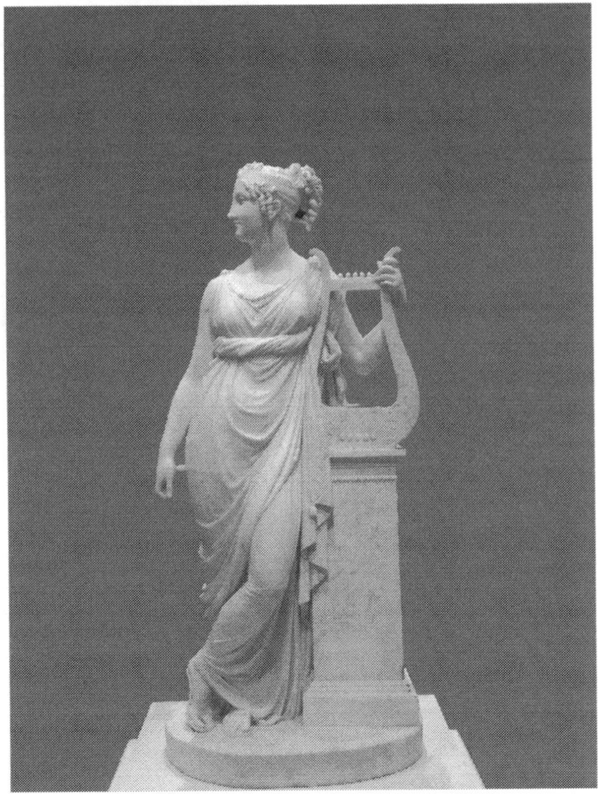

FIGURE 1 *Terpsichorn Lyran* (muse of lyric poetry)—1814–1816, marble.

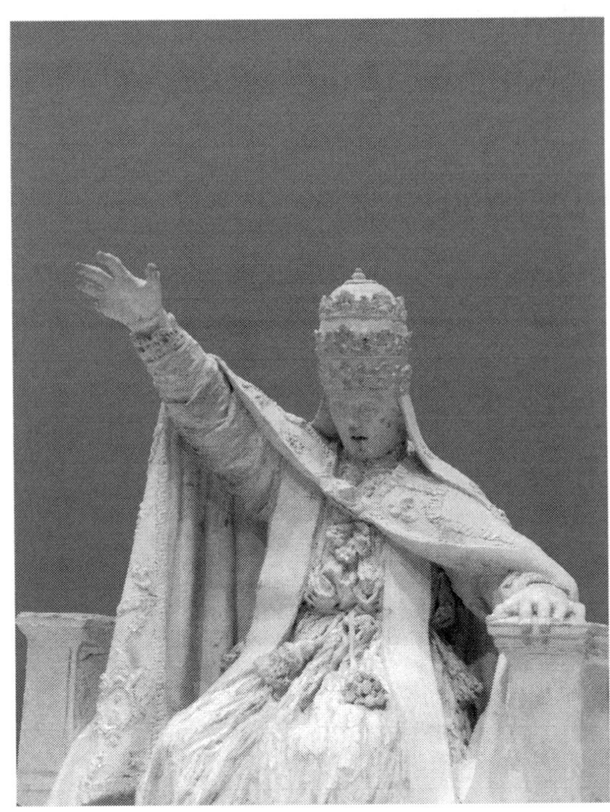

FIGURE 3 *Pope Clement XIV*—1793, terracotta.

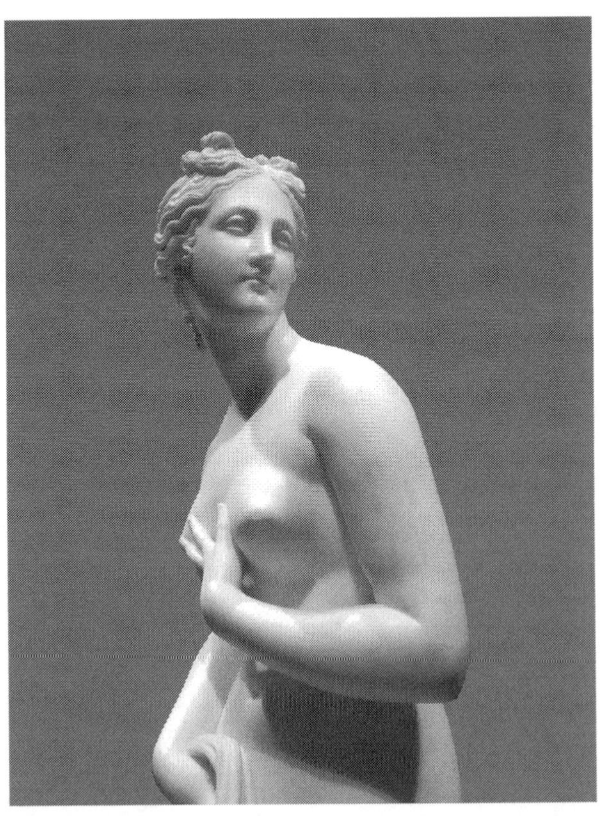

FIGURE 2 *Venus* (detail)—C 11757, marble.

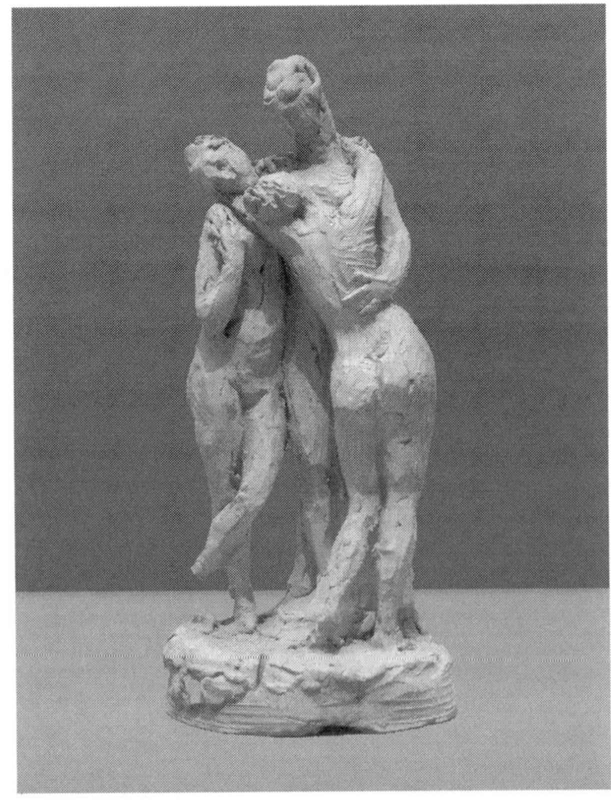

FIGURE 4 *The Three Graces* (version 1)—1812, terracotta.

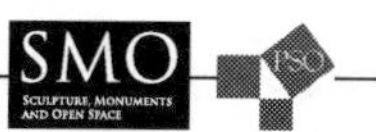

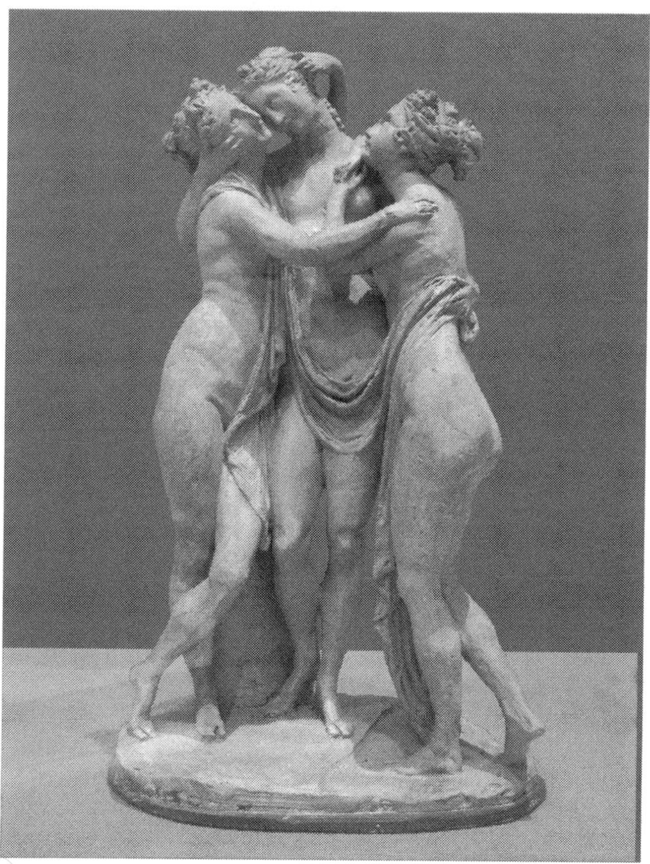

FIGURE 5 *The Three Graces* (version 2)—1812, terracotta.

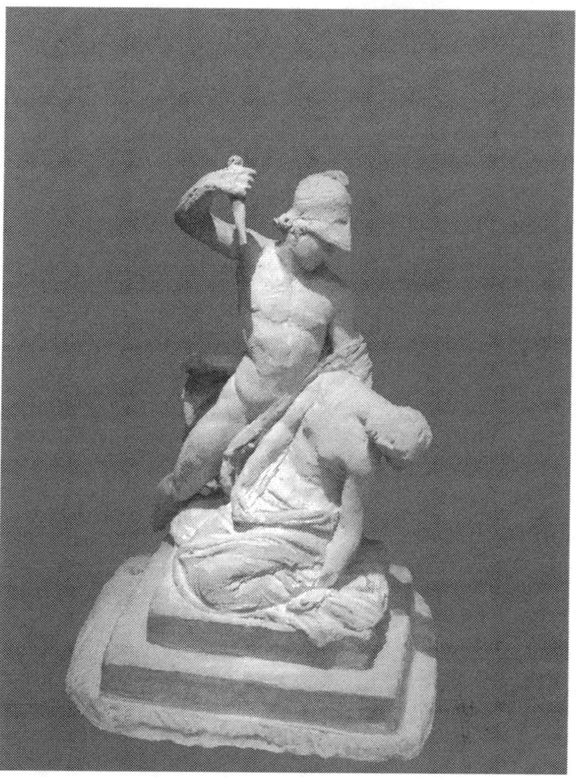

FIGURE 6 *Pyrrhus sacrificing polyxene* (version 1)—c. 1799, terracotta.

process that he used to help him envision and execute his sculpture (Figures 6 and 7). Most of his clay sketches were done quickly, and from the reports of those who were present during his modeling process—they reportedly could feel his intense focus and the emotions emanating from him as he sketched in the clay. And observing some of the clay sketches, such as *Adam and Eve, Mourning the Dead Abel*, it is possible to still see the fresh impression of his fingerprints he made in the process of creating them. The three different clay studies of *The Three Graces* that were also included in the exhibit, demonstrate how Canova explored the various stances he was considering before he finished the final marble sculptures. It is clear to see how valuable these clay sketches were for his process, as well as for him personally, as he often gave them as gifts to his most important clients. Some clay sketches are so visually powerful and expressive that one might imagine that if they had been exhibited during the late 20th century, they could have been accepted as serious examples of expressionistic sculpture (Figure 8).

One of the reasons the curators were able to secure so many complete clay and terracotta sculptures for the exhibit and provide depth and scholarship in the selection of objects, was due to the high esteem that was held for Canova and his work during his lifetime

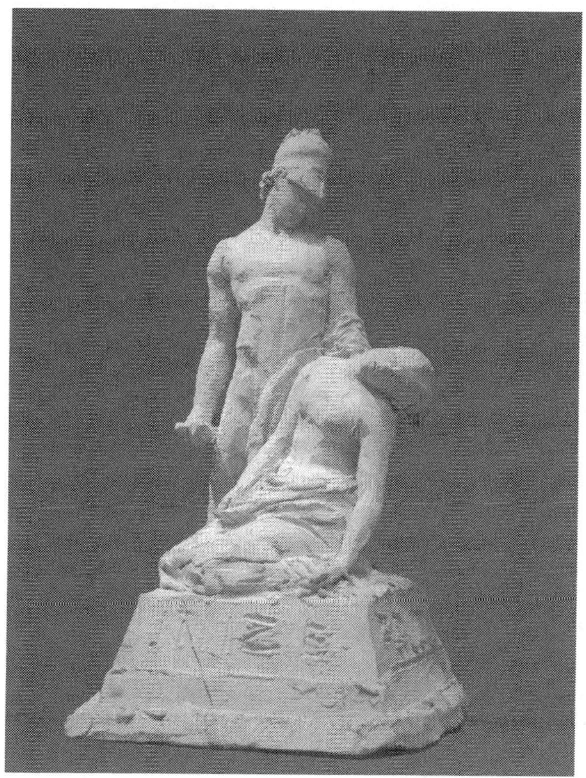

FIGURE 7 *Pyrrhus sacrificing polyxene* (version 2)—c. 1799, terracotta.

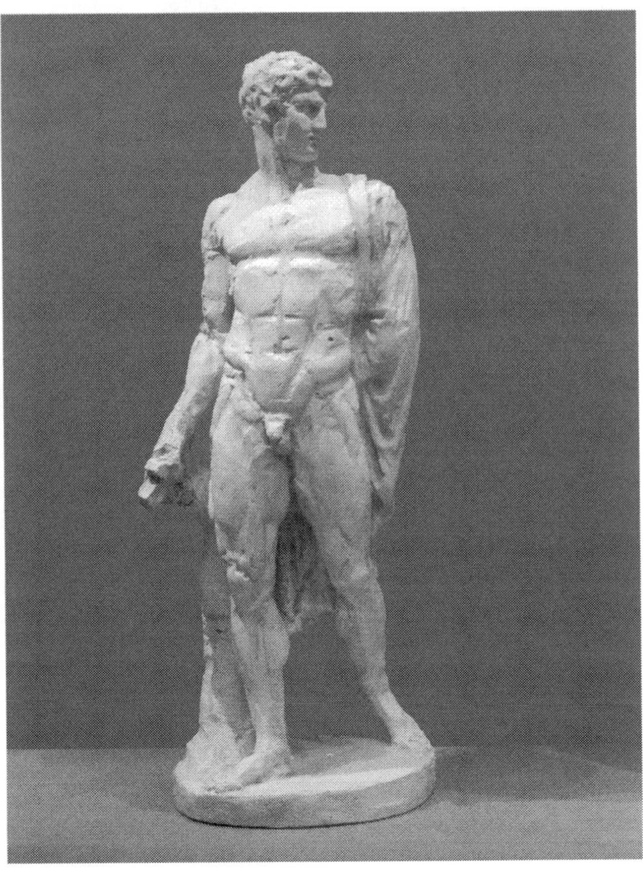

FIGURE 8 *Hector*—c. 1808, plaster.

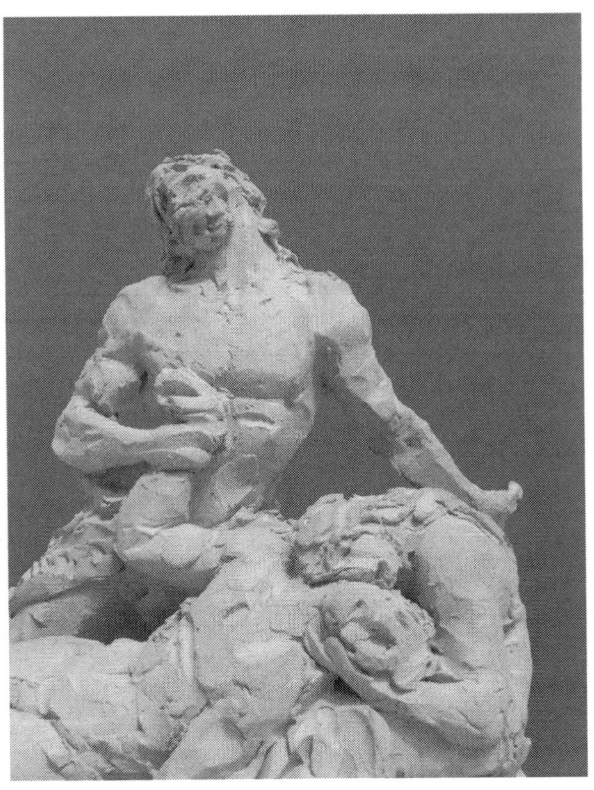

FIGURE 9 *Adam and Eve mourning the dead Abel* (version 1)—1818–1822, terracotta.

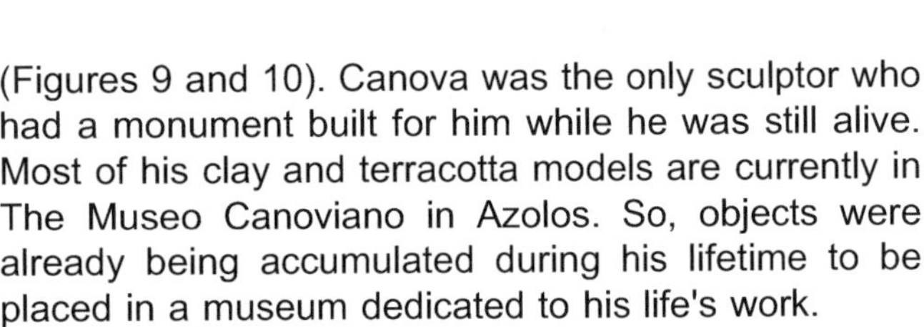

(Figures 9 and 10). Canova was the only sculptor who had a monument built for him while he was still alive. Most of his clay and terracotta models are currently in The Museo Canoviano in Azolos. So, objects were already being accumulated during his lifetime to be placed in a museum dedicated to his life's work.

Canova was born in Pessagno, Italy, which was part of the Venetian Republic in 1757. He experienced his father's death, who was also a sculptor, at the age of 3, and he was raised by his paternal grandfather, Pietro Canova, who owned a marble quarry and was also a stone mason and sculptor. In his youth, Canova demonstrated an unusual talent for modeling. There are even two small shrines carved in Carrara marble that he completed when he was only 9, that are still present in the museum in Passagno. After some of his work was seen by a wealthy aristocrat and collector, Giovanni Vallier, Vallier recommended that Canova be apprenticed to Giuseppe Bernardi.

So, at only 14 years of age, Canova left for Venice with Bernardi, but after only 2 years of studies in his workshop, Bernardi died. Canova then entered the workshop of Giovanni Ferrari. During this time in Venice, he was able to strengthen all of his skills—concentrating on his technique in terracotta and stone carving. After he left Ferrari, he attended the Academy

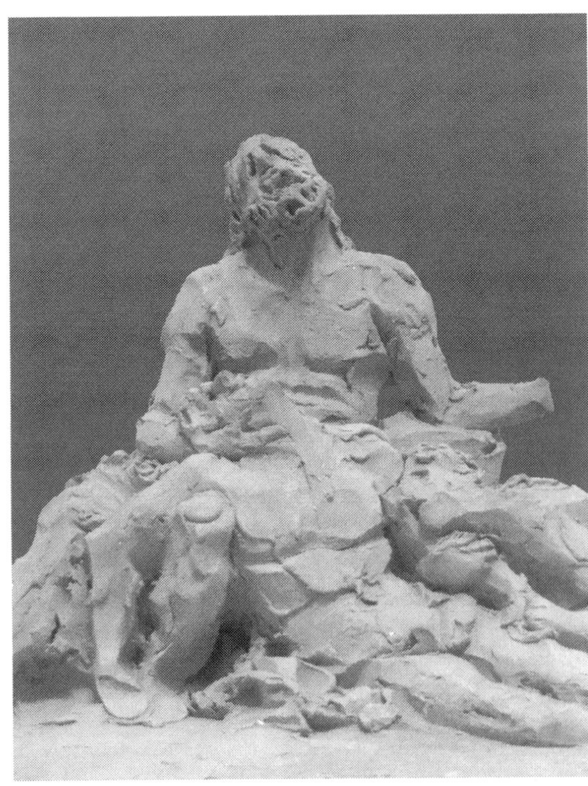

FIGURE 10 *Adam and Eve mourning the dead Abel* (version 2)—c. 1818, terracotta.

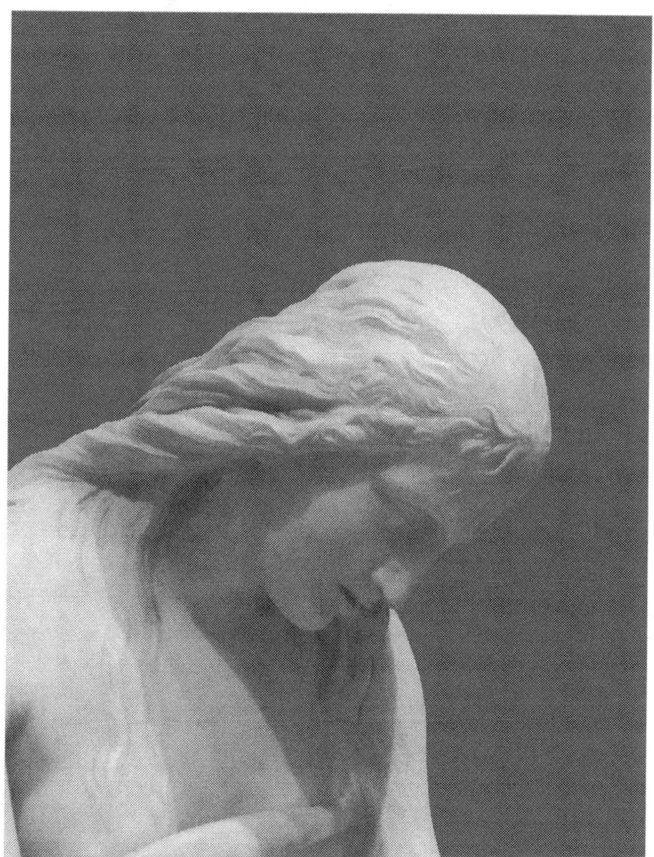

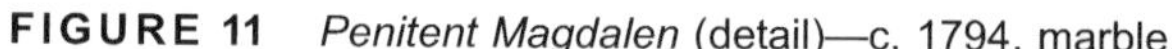

FIGURE 11 *Penitent Magdalen* (detail)—c. 1794, marble.

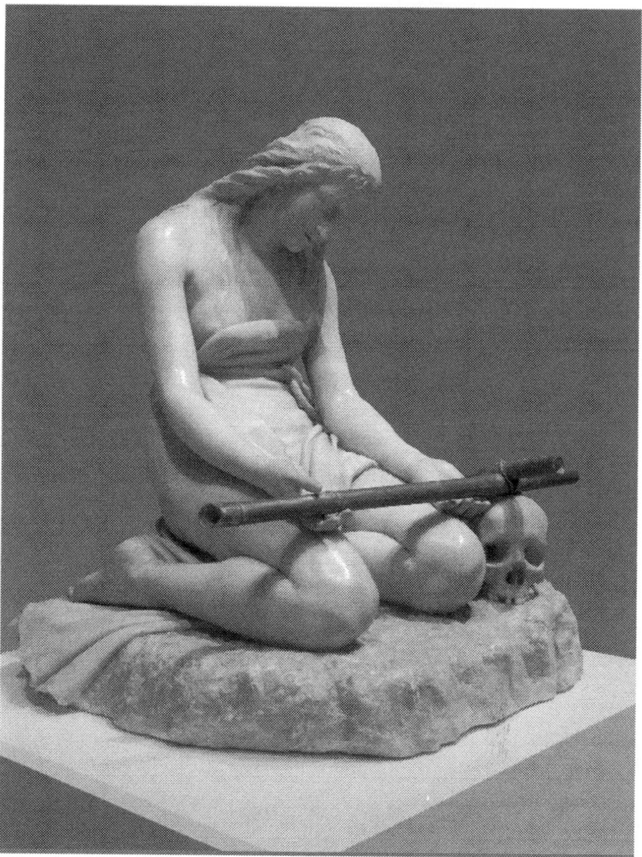

FIGURE 12 *Penitent Magdalen*—c. 1794, marble.

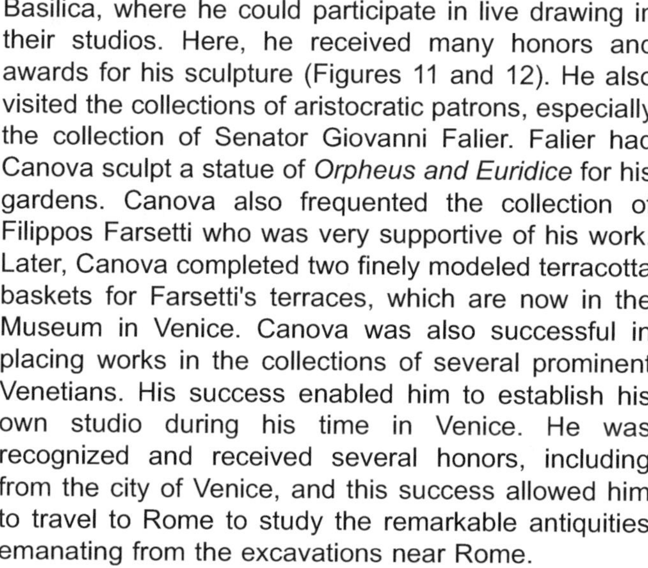

Basilica, where he could participate in live drawing in their studios. Here, he received many honors and awards for his sculpture (Figures 11 and 12). He also visited the collections of aristocratic patrons, especially the collection of Senator Giovanni Falier. Falier had Canova sculpt a statue of *Orpheus and Euridice* for his gardens. Canova also frequented the collection of Filippos Farsetti who was very supportive of his work. Later, Canova completed two finely modeled terracotta baskets for Farsetti's terraces, which are now in the Museum in Venice. Canova was also successful in placing works in the collections of several prominent Venetians. His success enabled him to establish his own studio during his time in Venice. He was recognized and received several honors, including from the city of Venice, and this success allowed him to travel to Rome to study the remarkable antiquities emanating from the excavations near Rome.

In 1780, Canova decided to move to Rome, and with the help of the Venetian Ambassador Girolano Zulcani's support, along with the aid of his friends in Venice, who applied for a 3-year stipend from Venice to support him, he was able to move to the city. After he arrived and set up his studio, initially in rooms at Zulcani's palace, Canova began to receive commissions, including an important sculpture, the *Theseus and the Minotaur*, which when it was first seen, was thought to be an original piece of ancient sculpture. Because of the stipend, he was able to study the work of the ancients, as well as make drawings of the works of Michelangelo. He was also able to take the time to attend lectures and workshops, where he could learn new techniques being studied, such as pointing, which was a new process designed to transfer information from a plaster model to a marble block. This new process made possible a much more accurate and easier process to complete a finished stone sculpture, which he was able to utilize in his studio and assign much of the initial work to his assistants.

While he was in Rome, his commissions started to expand, and he was able to hire a larger number of assistants, which also enabled him to complete more commissions (Figure 13). Eventually, he was successful enough to gain the attention of the Vatican, which gave him several projects, including direct commissions from the Pope. This success was swift and soon he was receiving commissions for his work from other parts of Europe (Figure 14). His *Cupid and Psyche* was acquired by a Scottish collector. And soon after, Napoleon, who had consolidated Italy into the Republic, became aware of his work and eventually became an active collector of his sculpture. In Rome, Canova

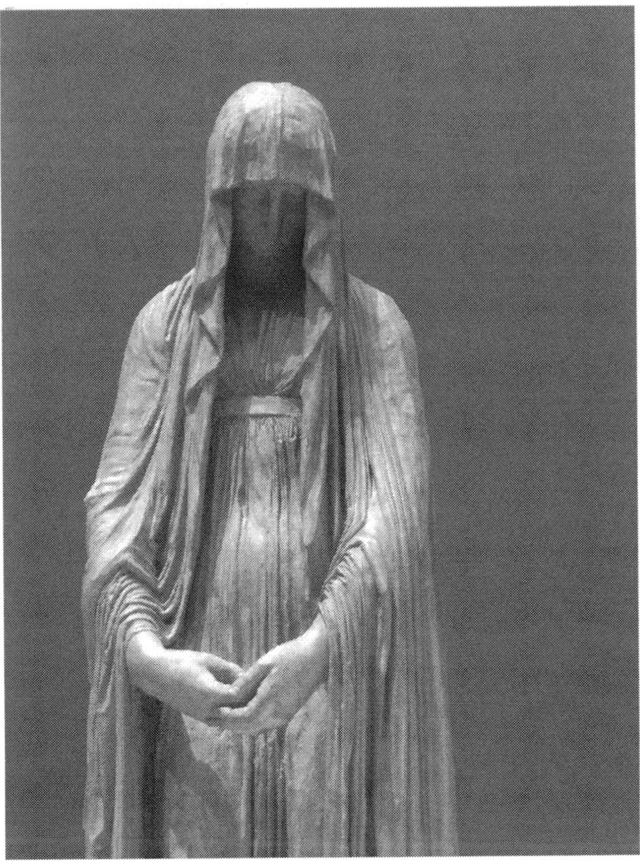

FIGURE 13 *Piety*—c. 1783, terracotta.

was able to complete a great number of commissions in his very active studio. He also began to perform diplomatic activities for the Vatican, and later in his career, to be recognized for his work in helping to return art that Napoleon had taken to France. While working for the Pope, he was able to complete several large and important projects, including one in Saint Peter's Basilica for Clement XIII. Through this, he received many honors and was inducted into many orders of chivalry. To influence his international clients, he had prints of his work distributed throughout Europe. Because of the extensive interest in his art and of his growing importance, several books were also being written about him and his sculpture, which extended his reputation that continued to grow throughout Europe. He eventually earned the respect and attention of the writers and poets, who began to express admiration for his art, especially Byron, who wrote expressively about his sculpture. Throughout his time in Rome, he continued to immerse himself in his work and complete several projects throughout Europe (Figure 15).

After many successful years in his studio in Rome. He eventually moved back to Passagno, primarily because of his increasingly poor health. Even there, he continued to immerse himself in his work and he was actively involved in many projects in the city, particularly with cultural activities (Figure 16). In 1822, Canova died in the house of a friend. It was an

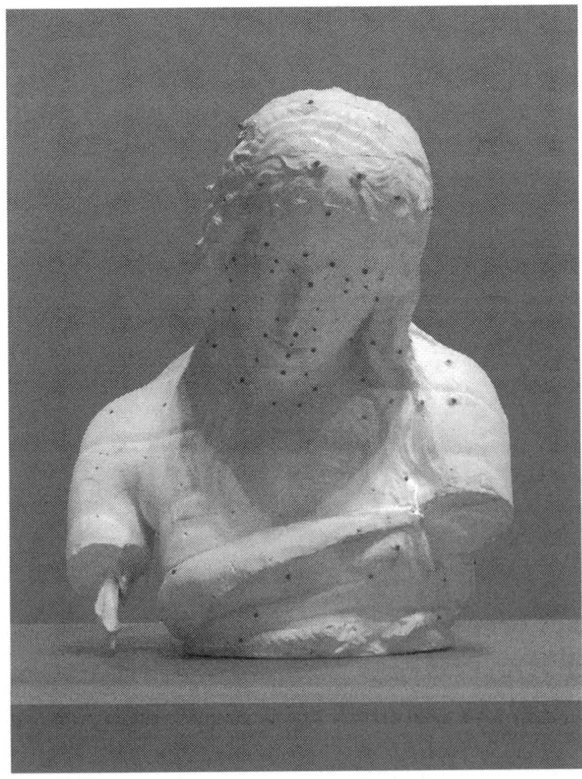

FIGURE 14 *Head of Penitent Magdalen*—c. 1794–1809, plaster with small metal tags used in the pointing process.

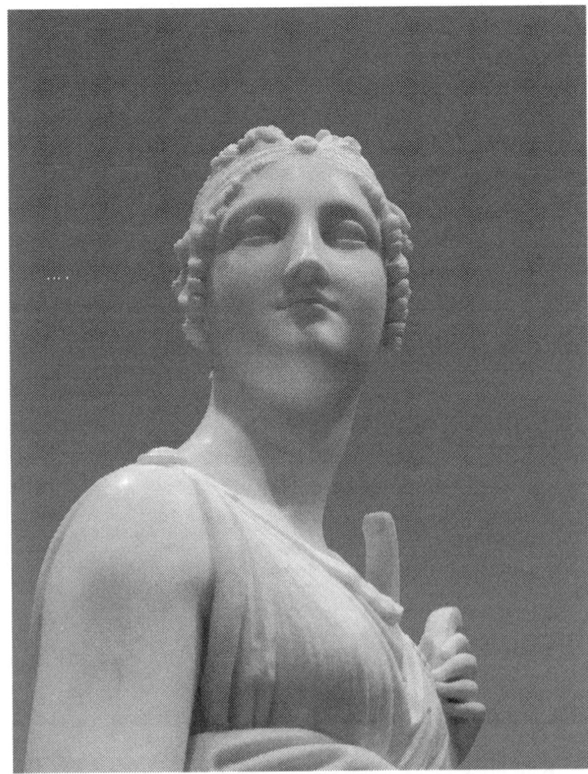

FIGURE 15 *Terpsichone Lyran* (muse of lyric poetry) detail—1814–1816, marble.

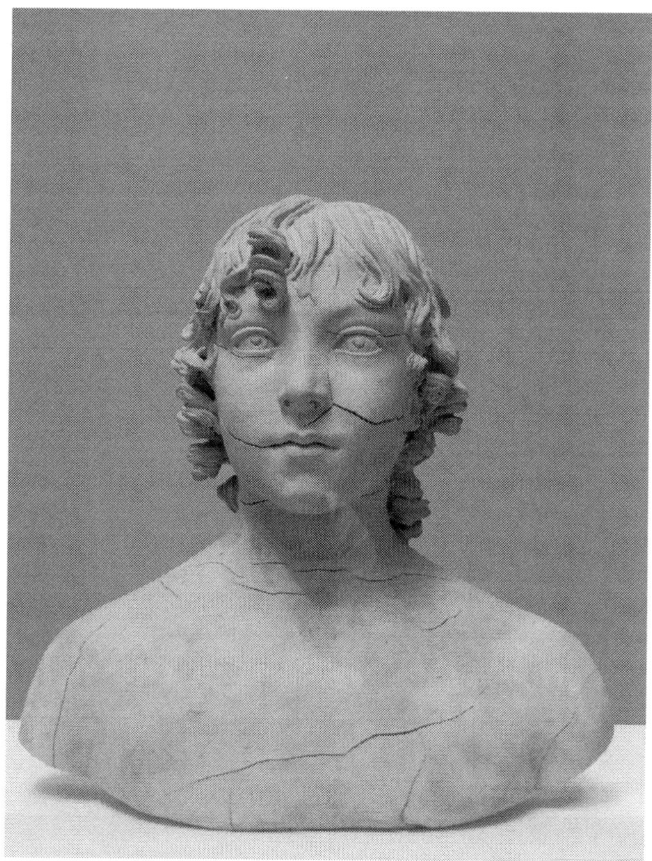

FIGURE 16 *Study of boy*—c. 1790, terracotta.

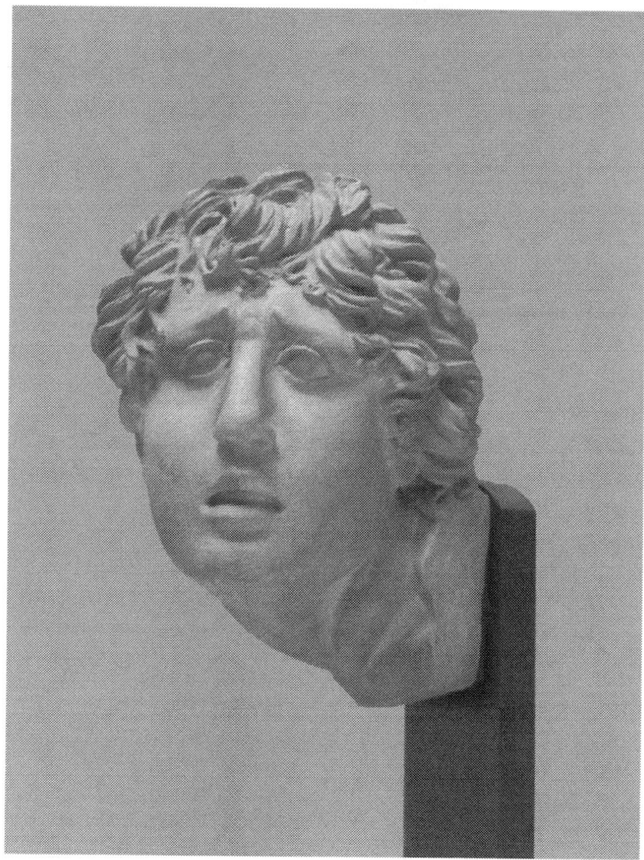

FIGURE 17 *Character head*—c. 1780, terracotta.

enormous loss to the art community and his life was mourned in the art communities of several capitals in Europe. His body was even treated as a relic, and heart was removed and placed in a museum collection and his right hand was placed in the art archives in Venice. His half-brother and executor to his estate made a great effort to ensure that all of the clay and terracotta models and his marble sculpture, as well as his tools, were removed from his studio in Rome in order that they could be set up in the museum celebrating his life's work (Figure 17).

While the highlight of the exhibition was his clay sketches and terracotta sculptures and models, there were actually 60 objects in the full exhibit. These included several completed and important marble sculptures, which revealed the precise and involved process Canova took to create the exquisite surfaces he was able to obtain on his finished pieces (Figure 18). While his assistants would block out areas of the sculpture, Canova always took a great deal of effort to complete the faces and other fleshy areas of his marbles himself, securing his reputation as not only a remarkably talented sculptor but an extremely skilled one as well.

While Canova was initially influenced by the Rococo period of art when he first arrived in Venice, he quickly established a renewed focus after studying the ancient sculptures being unearthed in Italy, which led to his leadership of the Neoclassic rise in the early 19th century. His contributions were significant, and his reputation and influence was felt throughout Europe. His leadership in this period of sculpture were legionary, and his concern for his fellow artists

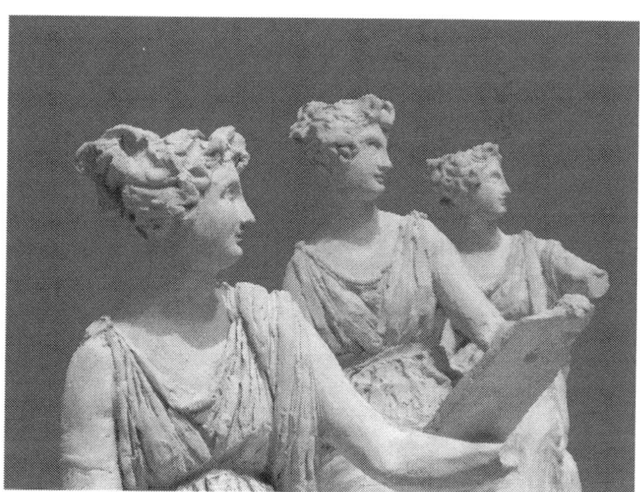

FIGURE 18 *Three female heads* (detail), marble.

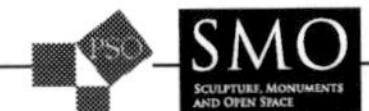

was deeply personal for him, as he gave a significant amount of his wealth to help younger artists and sent clients to struggling artists as well. The emergence of the powerful Romantic Age in Art began to dominate the 19th century, and his influence and importance were diminished. However, recent scholarship is beginning to recognize his influence and importance in the history of art, and this exhibition provides a significant insight and understanding of his genius and his major contributions to art.

Received: 9 May 2024 | Revised: 11 June 2024 | Accepted: 18 June 2024

DOI: 10.1002/smo3.12008

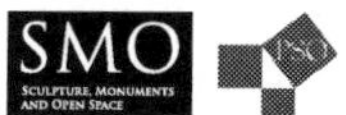

ARTICLE

Anne Olsen Daub: MULTI-FACETED

Gail Phinney

Freelance Writer, Los Angeles, California, USA

Correspondence
Gail Phinney, Freelance Writer, Los Angeles, CA, USA.
Email: gail.phinney@gmail.com

KEYWORDS
Anne Olsen Daub, craftsmanship, exhibition, sculpture

MULTI-FACETED, the title of San Pedro based artist Anne Olsen Daub's sculpture exhibition at the Palos Verdes Art Center in Rancho Palos Verdes, CA, references the quality of finished gemstones that are carefully cut to reveal their innermost beauty. It is also the perfect descriptor for this versatile fine artist, sculptor, and jewelry designer with an uncanny ability to spot the hidden potential in everyday objects and skillfully re-shape them into artworks of rare beauty (Figure 1).

Anne has been honing her unique design esthetic and impeccable craftsmanship since childhood when she first started creating jewelry out of beads and wire. Anne was only 12 when she sold her designs by consignment to a Costa Mesa drug store.

She would be thrilled to come back and find that someone actually purchased the pieces and she earned a few dollars. As a teenager, and aspiring artist living in Fresno, she longed to be a part of the LA scene.

Anne went on to attend Fresno City College for Fine Art and Otis College of Art and Design majoring in fashion design, which became her first career. From there she made her way to Mattel where she became a project designer, responsible for new doll concepts and fashions; including styles for the company's iconic Barbie.

Ultimately, she found herself in need of more fulfilling artistic expression. Stepping away from the corporate world enabled her to return to fine art and rediscover her passion for sculpture (Figure 2).

After leaving Mattel, Anne joined an LA assemblage group. There she discovered the joy of sourcing seemingly disparate materials and combining them together into a cohesive whole. Concerned about the marketability of those pieces and needing to support herself as an artist, she returned to making jewelry, which the artist describes as "mini one-of-a-kind assemblage pieces."

The concept of jewelry as sculpture became the inspiration for *MULTI-FACETED.* Originally conceived of as a show of wearable art, Anne pumped up the volume to create a uniquely original and wildly creative exhibition of large-scale, jewelry-inspired sculpture (Figure 3). She explains, "It gave me an opportunity to do something big. I like visual interest, things different sizes, different materials are visually interesting to me."

The desire to explore different materials tapped into another one of Anne's interests—sustainability. Finding herself with limited access to art supplies and surrounded by cardboard at her studio, she began experimenting with corrugated paper as an art medium during the pandemic.

The first iteration of that experimentation was the 2021 exhibit *Out of the Box* at Michael Stearns Studio @ The Loft. The work was inspired by the visual imagery of the 1939 film, *The Wizard of Oz,* and L. Frank Baum's original text, *The Land of Oz.* For Anne, corrugated paper became the perfect malleable medium to interpret the fantastical narrative.

The play of light on the larger-than-life low relief pieces created ominous shadows that established a sense of childlike wonder. The density of color achieved by the artist's use of highly pigmented Flashe paint gave visual weight to the objects that belied their lightweight nature.

With a background in fashion design and pattern making, Anne has an innate understanding of materials and how to use them to their best advantage.

All figures are courtesy of Eugene Daub.

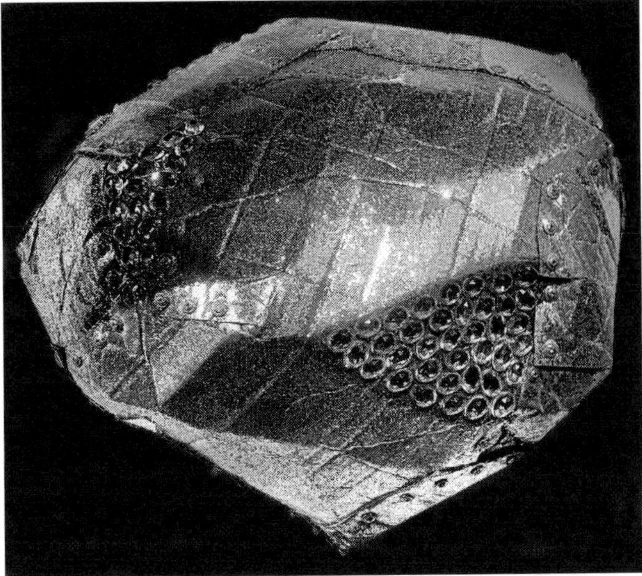

FIGURE 1 *Diamond in the Rough.* This *multifaceted* corrugated paper construction was inspired by raw uncut diamonds enhanced with highly reflective silver glitter and vintage cut glass gems showcasing its potential beauty when a diamond is fully cut.

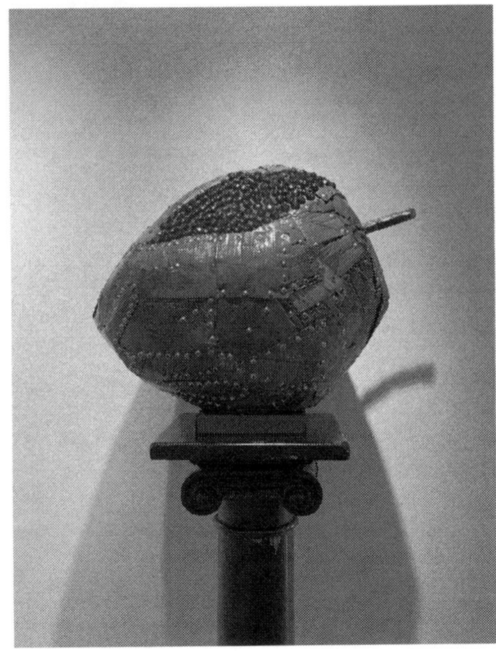

FIGURE 3 *Temptation.* The work challenged the artist to create a piece in-the-round spontaneously out of corrugated paper. *Temptation's* surface embellishments of vintage cut glass stones make for an alluring candy apple red center.

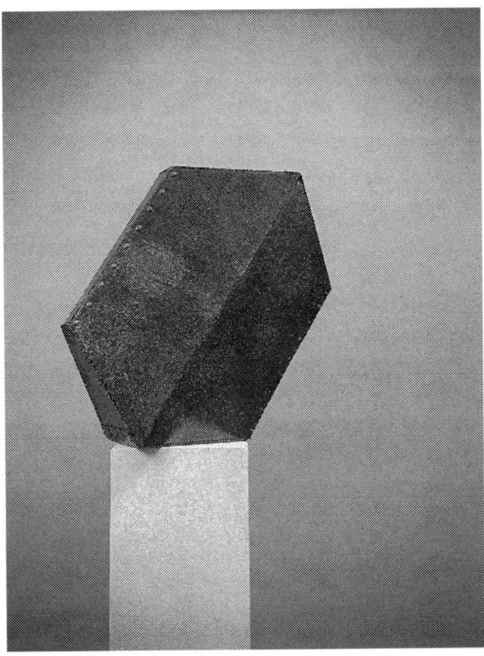

FIGURE 2 *Tourmaline.* A simple cut gem made to heroic proportions was an opportunity to explore color. Painting corrugated paper with pinks, reds, and purple glitter created dazzling surface and faceted effects.

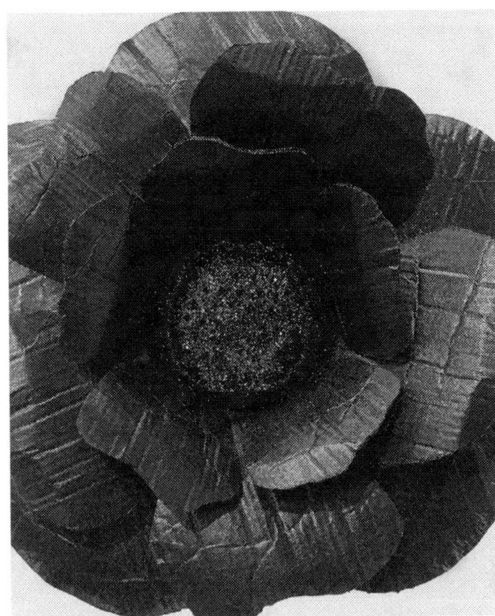

FIGURE 4 *Coco.* An oversized black flower inspired by silk flower pendants, the midnight blue glittery spiky center is mysterious and dangerous in its beauty. Its stamen are sharp screws pointed toward the viewer.

Corrugated paper can be manipulated into a glittering or metal-like surface; it can simulate wood, stone, and other sculptural materials. Additionally, the qualities of the material—lightweight, sustainable, strong, and long lasting—make it an ethical, as well as a practical choice (Figure 4).

Anne applied these same sensibilities to the construction of the work for the exhibition, *MULTI-FACETED*, created in 2023. There is a bold economy and honesty to the fabrication of each piece. Fasteners for such pieces as the up-scaled handbag titled *Canal*

Street and the larger-than-life ring called *Veritas* were selected for both their functional and decorative value. No opportunity for surface enhancement was wasted. No detail left undone. While the overall effect reads high design with a hint of whimsy, it is the craftsmanship that shines.

Still learning how to manipulate cardboard into desired shapes, Anne insists she wasn't seeking perfection. She believes, "Nothing's perfect. Nothing is measured with a ruler to make it perfect. I like imperfections. I like things that look like they are handmade."

Embracing imperfection, Anne works intuitively letting the materials tell her where they want to go. That was certainly the case with the mixed-media sculpture *Kryptonite and Pearls* (Figures 5 and 6). The artist's intention was to make a big faceted gem of some sort. She relates, "At first it started out black, but black wasn't working, and I thought, it needs to be green."

The process began with a layer of shellac to give the corrugated paper some strength, then paint, and finally Varathane polyurethane with painted glitter for added depth of dimension and maximum sparkle. The beads that form the necklace are big wooden balls painted with a pearlized paint. A repurposed pulley with a rich, rusted patina completes the look.

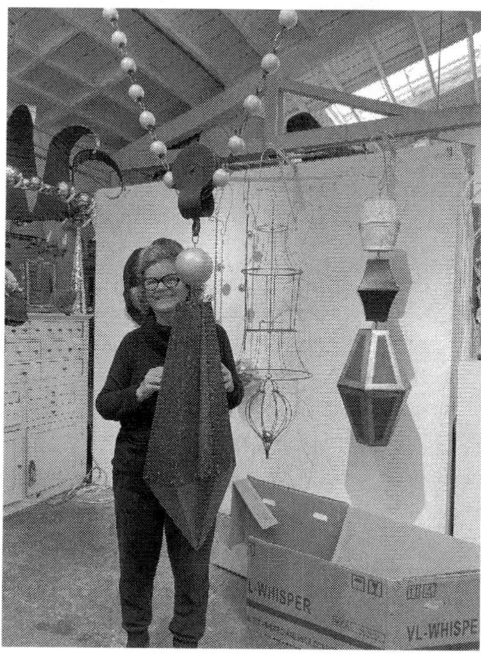

FIGURE 6 Anne in her studio next to *Kryptonite and Pearls.* To her right are a pair of giant earrings assembled from old lampshade frames.

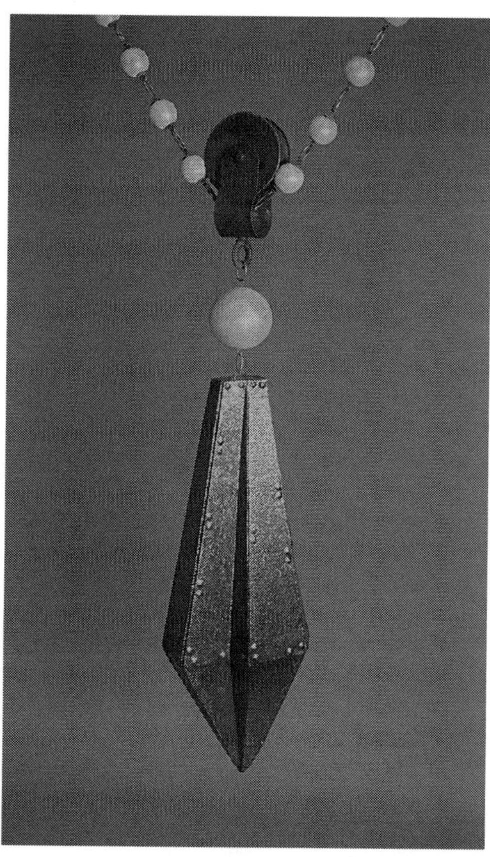

FIGURE 5 *Kryptonite and Pearls.* This giant necklace was inspired by one of the artist's favorite colors, deep emerald green. The green cut gem is corrugated paper painted in glitter. The wood pearls are covered with iridescent paint and held together with chandelier chain. Its center is an old barn pulley found on eBay.

A student of history, Anne believes that jewelry encapsulates an expression of its era. She is a proponent of the power of storytelling and jewelry's ability to carry profound messages. Such is the case with her series of sculptures inspired by posy rings.

Posy rings acquired their name from the French word poésie meaning poetry. These rings were popular from the late Medieval Period onwards reaching their height in the Victorian era. The rings were inscribed with secret messages of love between the giver and the recipient. The phrases were often written in Old French, Latin, or Old English.

Seduced by the allure of found objects, the artist has amassed a treasure trove of materials waiting to be repurposed. She recollects, "I have had these barrel stays that go around wine barrels for years and I've moved them around my studio wondering, 'What am I going to do with these things?'" So when the show came up she thought, "They're going to be rings!"

Drawn to the hidden messages in posy rings, the artist decided to emulate them in sculpture. *Meet Me at Midnight* was inspired by an actual posy ring message she found compelling. Layers of blue and black Flashe

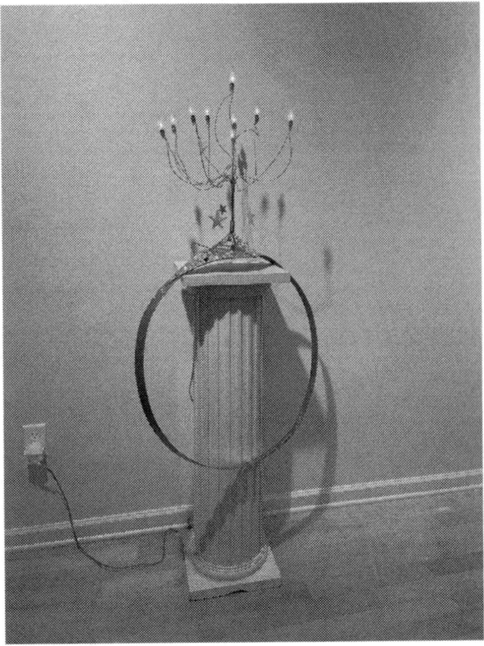

FIGURE 7 *Those Who Wander are Not Lost.* One of a four-ring series inspired by Victorian posey rings. A visual metaphor about exploration and discovery, the illuminated vintage candelabra creates a fantasy childlike effect.

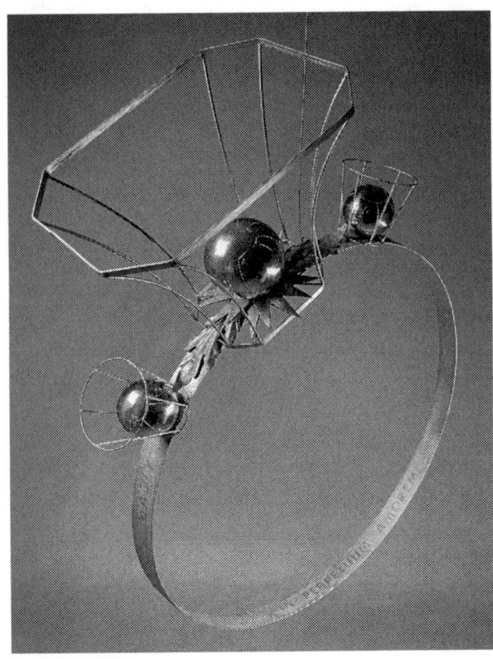

FIGURE 8 *Madly Deeply.* The mirror-like stainless balls act as diamonds reflecting both the giver and wearer receiving the secret message. The lettering on the inside band reads, "IN PERPETUUM AMOREM."

paint simulate the deep midnight blue color of a night sky with sprinkles of glitter evoking stars, resulting in a work that is as romantic and mysterious as the inscribed invitation.

Another posy ring inspired piece, *Those Who Wander* (Figure 7) holds personal meaning to the artist who relates to the notion that she also wanders at times, but never feels lost and includes a chandelier adornment to guide the way. While *Madly Deeply*, in the shape of a solitaire engagement ring with metal lampshade frames forming the silhouette of diamonds uses the Latin phrase, "in perpetuum amorem," meaning love forever (Figure 8).

Other objects in the show combine art and text, such as *The Jester,* a corrugated paper and mixed media crown, the inside of which features the line, "Heavy is the head that wears the crown," a popular reinterpretation of a quote from Shakespeare's play *Henry IV, Part 2*.

The artist shares, "I like stories, depth, and images that make you think." To that end, she has created an evocative series of antique mirrors collaged on the back with images saved from magazines and newspapers. The mirrors themselves have been collected from antique stores or have been gifted.

Stories We Tell explores the power of stories we read in childhood to form us by combining fairy tale imagery with a quote from Salman Rushdie's New York Times article on the subject, "The Stories We Love, Make Us Who We Are."

Adam Was features depictions of Adam and Eve from a Christopher Knight Los Angeles Times article about Lucas Cranach the Elder's famous panel paintings of the pair. In *Some Look,* the viewer is reflected back in an antique convex mirror, the frame above bearing the words, "Many look very few see," hand beaded onto pink velvet. In homage, perhaps, to the Evil Queen's magic mirror in the fairy tale *Snow White* and a commentary on the false sense of beauty we hold onto.

Another source of inspiration for the artist is the beauty of nature, out of which came the design concept for the necklace sculpture, *Gold Leaves.* The chain is fashioned from jacaranda tree trimmings hand painted in gold. Flat glass floral pebbles applied to corrugated paper Egyptian-style leaves emulate early morning dew.

The gem-like bugs that animate this piece were inspired by the art of French architect Thierry Despont. Best know for his restoration of the Statue of Liberty, Despont is equally admired for his exquisite insect assemblages made from found objects.

Rounding out the exhibition are wearable pieces, albeit oversized, that both call attention to Anne's background in fashion and convey significant meaning. The appropriately titled *Cruel Fashion* is a remarkable neckpiece displayed inside a wooden shadow box

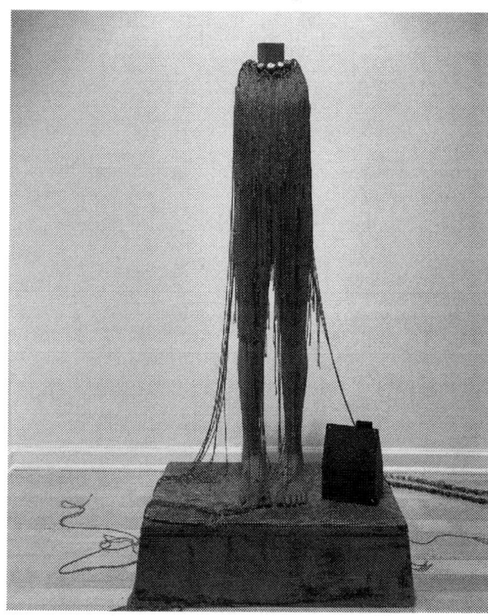

FIGURE 9 *Remembrance*. All hand strung, long red string elements with gold wood beads in front connect to 40 foot lengths of wood beads and found objects in back. The sculpture is about childhood memories dragged into adulthood.

consisting of a vintage leopard collar with faux pearls and antique thread spools. Her use of red crystals to emulate drops of blood makes a strong political statement about the industry's use of exotic furs.

Remembrance (Figure 9) is a powerfully symbolic vignette about the emotional weight of childhood memory we carry into adulthood. A cascading necklace consisting of full-length strands of red nylon cord is draped on a wooden sculpture of a youth; a self-portrait gifted to Anne by fellow artist Tom Van Sant. The sculpture is mounted on a distressed box, a black corrugated paper house at its feet. Behind it a heavy chain of wood beads and found objects extends down from the collar and snakes across the gallery floor.

Finally, showcasing her achievements as a jewelry designer are her mini one-of-a-kind assemblage pieces floating on a transparent glass table held captive under individual bell jars. The effect is nothing short of magical.

Anne Olsen Daub: MULTI-FACETED on view at Palos Verdes Art Center January 27 through April 13, 2024.

Received: 14 May 2024 | Accepted: 17 June 2024
DOI: 10.1002/smo3.12007

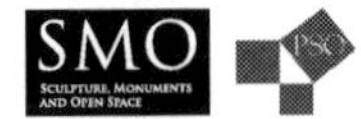

ARTICLE

Shaping the West

Blaine Smith

National Cowboy Museum, Oklahoma City, Oklahoma, USA

Correspondence
Blaine Smith, National Cowboy Museum, Oklahoma City, OK, USA.
Email: bsmith@nationalcowboymuseum.org

KEYWORDS
art; awards; exhibition; National Cowboy Museum; sculpture

The *Prix de West Invitational Art Exhibition & Sale* at the National Cowboy & Western Heritage Museum in Oklahoma City has, for a half-century, remained the world's preeminent Western-themed art show, each year featuring upward of 90 of the most celebrated painters and sculptors in North America, including several new guest artists annually. Although some art-world snobs might consider the concept of a “Western” art exhibition trite, the artwork of *Prix de West* reflects a level of skill, height of creativity, and nuance of viewpoint unsurpassed at any other exhibition of its size, Western-themed or not.

More than five decades since *Prix de West*'s debut, the artwork remains novel, surprising, and fresh despite all sharing a common (though admittedly vast) setting: the West. Regardless of one's gender, age, race, place of origin, or preconceptions toward “Western” art, the themes reflected in the artwork found in the exhibition are universal, meaning everyone can find a connection to the pieces if they try.

“*Prix de West* represents the best work of my most skilled contemporaries,” said sculptor and 2023 *Prix de West* Purchase Award recipient Walter T. Matia (Figure 1)—an opinion shared by 2023 *Prix de West* Buyers' Choice and James Earle Fraser Sculpture Award winner John Coleman. “My peers and collectors alike would probably agree that *Prix de West* is the flagship of all Museum art shows,” Coleman said. “Being invited to this prestigious venue is definitely a great honor.”

Like any great art, the works in *Prix de West* oftentimes surpass all descriptors—including Western, landscape, wildlife, abstract, and so on—to express a powerful feeling. The following sculptures not only captured something beyond words, but they also captured honors at the 2023 *Prix de West.*

Walter T. Matia, *Molly is a Working Girl*
Prix de West Purchase Award

A fellow of the National Sculpture Society and 30-year veteran of *Prix de West*, Walter T. Matia of Dickerson, Maryland, worked for the Nature Conservancy for more than a decade before he began sculpting full time. Matia initially focused his artwork on bird life, but in time expanded his themes to include sporting dogs and other animals (Figure 2). Today, these same creatures remain important subjects to Matia; consider his 2023 *Prix de West* works—three depict Western fowl, including a nearly three-foot-tall golden eagle titled *West with the Night*, while his Purchase Award-winning bronze *Molly is a Working Girl* portrays a bird dog sitting among cattails, watching over a duck it has retrieved (Figure 3).

“The ‘West’ I chose to focus on is its hunting and fishing, nonconsumptive recreational pursuits,” Matia said. “Financially and politically, these activities are changing much of Western culture. I have expressed these thoughts to many on the (*Prix de West*) Committee, and I think their consideration of *Molly is a Working Girl* was an acknowledgement of the importance of recreational activity in shaping the narrative of the new West,” he said.

Many might consider Matia's golden eagle sculpture *West with the Night* (Figure 4) a more likely contender for the *Prix de West* Purchase Award—the artist

Sculpture made a strong showing at the 2023 *Prix de West Invitational Art Exhibition & Sale*, claiming several of the exhibition's top prizes—including the coveted Purchase Award.

All figures are courtesy of National Cowboy Museum.

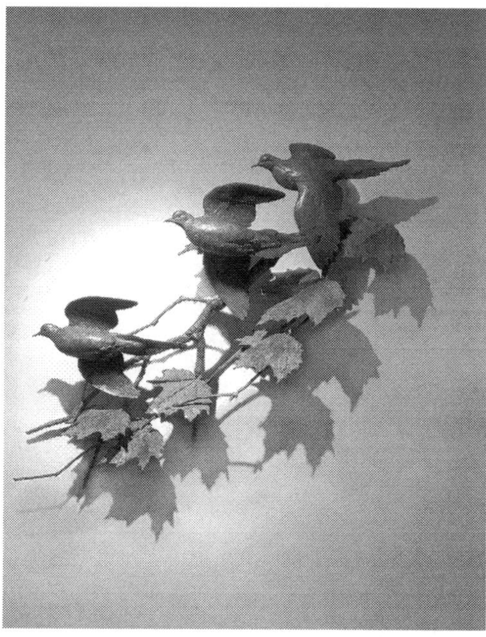

FIGURE 1 Walter T. Matia, *Fall Flight,* Bronze, 21″ H × 35″ W × 11½″ D. 2023 *Prix de West Invitational Art Exhibition & Sale.*

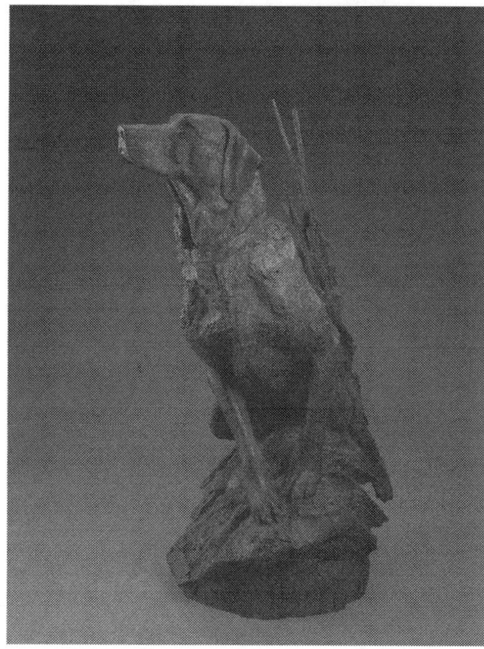

FIGURE 3 Walter T. Matia, *Molly is a Working Girl*, Bronze, 38″ H × 25″ W × 16½″ D. 2023 *Prix de West Invitational Art Exhibition & Sale.*

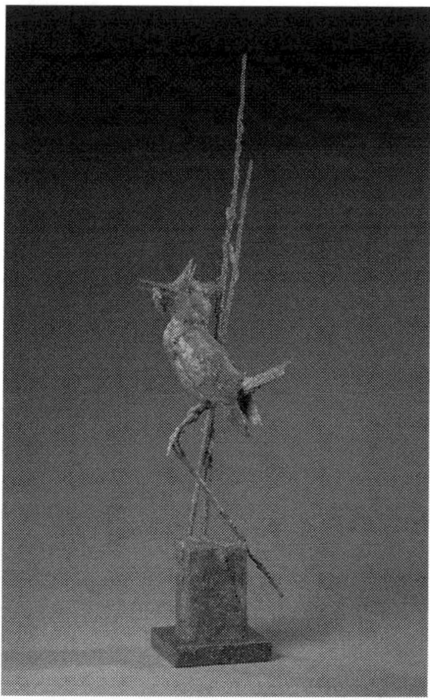

FIGURE 2 Walter T. Matia, *The Fisher King,* Bronze, 31½″ H × 8¾″ W × 7¼″ D. 2023 *Prix de West Invitational Art Exhibition & Sale.*

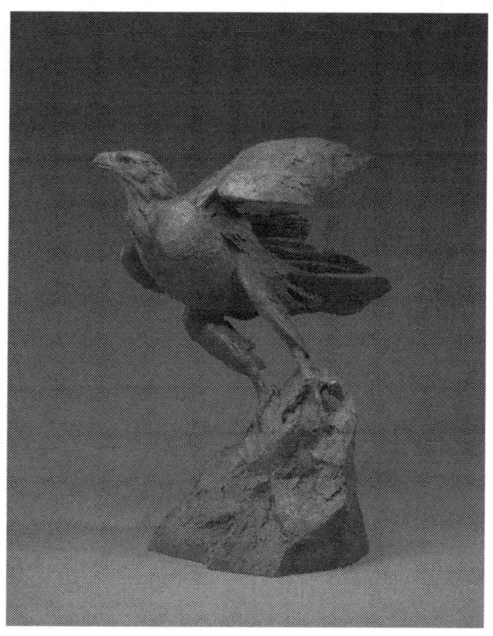

FIGURE 4 Walter T. Matia, *West with the Night*, Bronze, 33″ H × 24″ W × 22½″ D. 2023 *Prix de West Invitational Art Exhibition & Sale.*

himself believes it would have been an easier choice. With the Purchase Award going to *Molly is a Working Girl*, however, Matia is "proud and gratified the Committee chose to look more expansively at the subject matter that should be included in the wonderful *Prix de West* permanent collection."

Established in 1973—the first year of what was then officially known as the National Academy of Western Art and later changed to *Prix de West*—the *Prix de West* Purchase Award is given each year to the piece judged best in show, which is then purchased for the National Cowboy Museum's permanent collection. Today, the Museum's *Prix de West* Collection is considered one of the finest contemporary Western art collections assembled, and to this, Matia's *Molly is a Working Girl* was added in 2023.

"My subjects are slightly different from many of the artists in the show," Matia said. "I am interested in Western wildlife and the Western wildlife experience, but I don't have much experience with classical big game. I don't have much to say about elk or moose, bison nor bears. I don't see them enough to know the gestures and situations that are 'sculptural.'"

"I live in Maryland, where turkeys are big game," he said. "I hunt and fish, bird watch and botanize out West—blackbirds, green herons, kingfishers and trout and cattails fill my thoughts. Bird dogs and retrievers, waterfowl and game birds provide many of the artistic situations of my time in the West."

"The 'West' is no one thing and this is where things get very complicated," Matia said. "There is a diverse history and there is an equally diverse and evolving present. Its historic cultures have clashed, and much of the art in [*Prix de West*] speaks to that history. Its landscapes retain both majesty and the scars of development and resource use," he said. "… I am an artist, but I am also a scientist and conservationist. One person sees a painting of cattle being driven across a stream, and they see a powerful tradition and skill—as do I, but there is also a cringe in my soul as I also see a denuded stream bank and muddied water … it's not just one thing."

To find, among all the disparate works of art exhibited at each *Prix de West*, a single work on which to bestow the title of best of show and to include as part of the world's premier collection of contemporary Western art must, no doubt, be daunting. This task falls, in part, to Susan Roeder, National Cowboy Museum Board member and chair of the *Prix de West* Committee.

"Within the deliberation process for the *Prix de West* Purchase Award, we look for an artwork that is among the very best that has been brought to the exhibition," Roeder said. "Yet, holistically, we are also considering a work that is among the very best the individual artist has ever exhibited and, importantly, a work that says something new or that allows the National Cowboy Museum to expand the story it tells of the American West throughout history."

"In the case of *Molly is a Working Girl*, we see an exquisitely sculpted bird dog from Matia, without a doubt our nation's premier sculptor of hunting dogs and game birds," she said, "and we can take a moment to ponder the importance that bird hunting in the West has played in feeding countless families during hard times; in fostering camaraderie among hunters in thousands of duck blinds or in open prairie across the land through the ages; in the bond of trust that is formed between a hunter and a faithful dog; and in the tradition that is most typically passed down from a father to a son as a rite of passage."

"Bird hunting and bird dogs have a ubiquitous presence in the annals of Western history through today," Roeder said, "and we were not fully telling that story before *Molly* was chosen to be a gorgeous representation of those ideals."

John Coleman, *Warrior Spirit, Crazy Horse* Buyers' Choice Award and James Earle Fraser Sculpture Award

Prescott, Arizona, based sculptor and painter John Coleman has been a *Prix de West* participating artist for 17 years. A National Sculpture Society fellow and Cowboy Artists of America member, Coleman's bronzes, oil paintings, and charcoal drawings often depict Native American subjects. When his monumental sculpture *Warrior Spirit, Crazy Horse* (Figure 5), received both the Buyers' Choice Award and the James Earle Fraser Sculpture Award at the 2023 *Prix de West*, it marked the third time that a Coleman sculpture received these two awards simultaneously; it also marked Coleman's fourth Buyers' Choice Award win.

Each year, the *Prix de West* Buyers' Choice Award is chosen by *Prix de West* attendees via popular vote; the James Earle Fraser Award is given to the sculpture that most exhibits exceptional artistic merit while capturing the spirit of the West as exemplified in the works of iconic twentieth-century American sculptor James Earle Fraser.

To capture the accolades of a majority of both patrons and judges with a single work—and to do it three times over, no less, as Coleman has—is no mean feat. Yet, when one beholds *Warrior Spirit,*

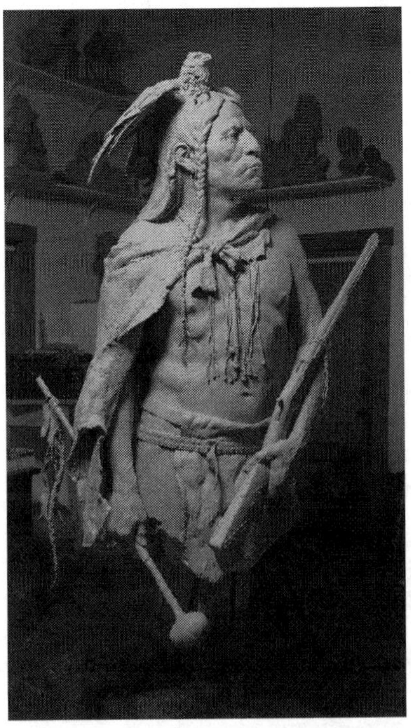

FIGURE 5 John Coleman, *Warrior Spirit, Crazy Horse*, Clay, 33″ H × 24″ W × 22½″ D. 2023 *Prix de West Invitational Art Exhibition & Sale.*

*Crazy Horse*in person, the power inherent in this 8-foot-plus bust of the famed Lakota warrior is undeniable.

"The stories of Native Americans have been the subject of my work since the beginning of my career and I think of these stories as American mythology," Coleman said. "It's important to me as a non-native American to view the historical context as an outsider and using historical documents as metaphors for what I consider to be a more universal meaning that we as Americans all share."

"For *Warrior Spirit, Crazy Horse*, I found an opportunity to present a sculpture of great power," he said. "For Native Americans, Crazy Horse was a dominant hero. Never having been photographed, I used stories and photos of his descendants to create his likeness, and for this particular piece monumental scale is very important. In a time like this where we celebrate superheroes, Crazy Horse, I feel, exemplifies that concept."

"I took the historic documents describing his nature and fleshed out what I felt portrayed what he might have looked like and the essence of a great warrior," Coleman said. "The key to this goes beyond illustrating what a piece may be based on, and I believe this particular sculpture owes a lot of its success to its design, which ultimately is most important."

"This sculpture is in a bust format, creating a diamond shape where his torso appears to be floating as in a vignette of one of my charcoal drawings," he said. "For such a large piece, this was a little risky, but by doing this I was able to bring the core of the design closer to the audience. Had I included his entire body," he said, "the piece would have been over 11 feet tall, and I believe the design wouldn't have been as intriguing."

Said Roeder, "John Coleman is simply in a class by himself in sculpting Plains Indians, and has won the James Earle Fraser award multiple times. In the case of his monumental *Crazy Horse*, it is a bold masterwork that was impossible to not choose for the sculpture award, and so, rightfully won the award, hands down, after very little discussion."

"I was delighted to learn that it sold to a first time *Prix de West* attendee!" she said. "Talk about beginner's luck!"

Blair Buswell, *Risky Business*; Hey, Over HERE!!!; and *Showtime*

Express Ranches Great American Cowboy Award

A fellow and former board member of the National Sculpture Society, Blair Buswell of Utah has participated in *Prix de West* for 28 years. Regarded as a master portrait artist, Buswell has sculpted more than 110 busts of Pro Football Hall of Fame inductees since 1983. In 2011, he received the *Prix de West* James Earle Fraser Sculpture Award.

In 2023, Buswell submitted three rodeo clown-themed bronzes to *Prix de West —Risky Business* (Figure 6), depicting a rodeo clown attempting to escape the horns of a pursuing bull; *Hey, Over HERE!!!* (Figure 7), showing two rodeo clowns taunting an unseen bull from the cover of a barrel; and *Showtime* (Figure 8), which features the bust of a rodeo clown who is ready to entertain the crowd.

Altogether, Buswell's three bullfighter bronzes were awarded the *Prix de West* Express Ranches Great American Cowboy Award, which is awarded annually to the finest portrayal of cowboy subject matter, be it a painting, sculpture, or drawing.

In describing *Risky Business*, the work among his three pieces that were featured in the 2023 *Prix de West*

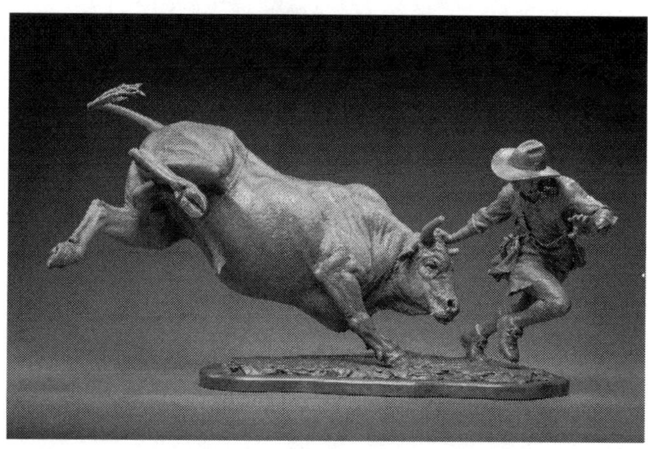

FIGURE 6 Blair Buswell, *Risky Business*, Bronze, 18″ H × 33″ W × 15″ D. 2023 *Prix de West Invitational Art Exhibition & Sale*.

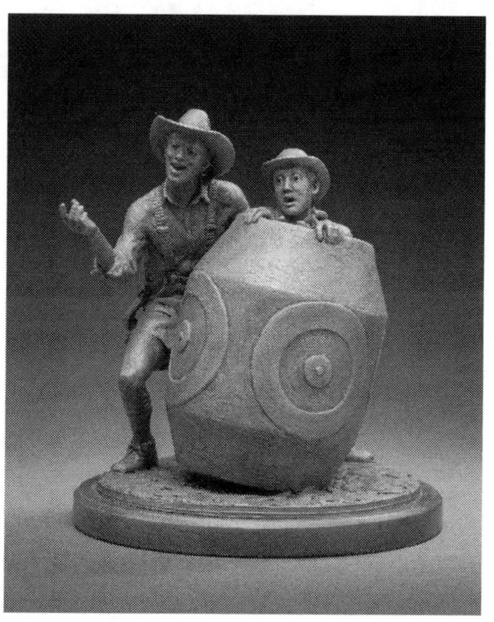

FIGURE 7 Blair Buswell, *Hey, Over HERE!!!*, Bronze, 11″ H × 10″ W × 10″ D. 2023 *Prix de West Invitational Art Exhibition & Sale*.

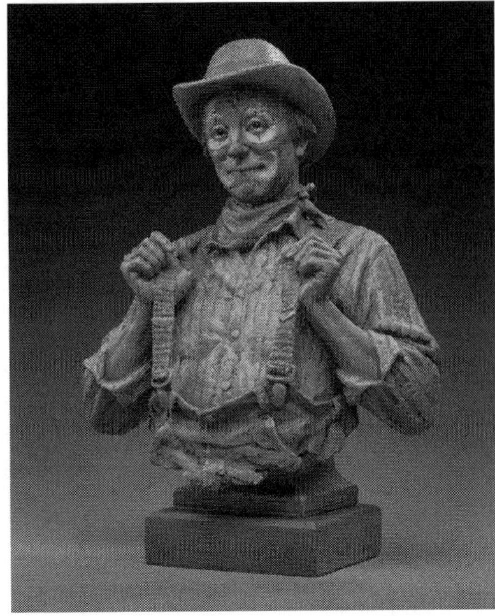

FIGURE 8 Blair Buswell, *Showtime*, Bronze, 15″ H × 11″ W × 7″ D. 2023 *Prix de West Invitational Art Exhibition & Sale.*

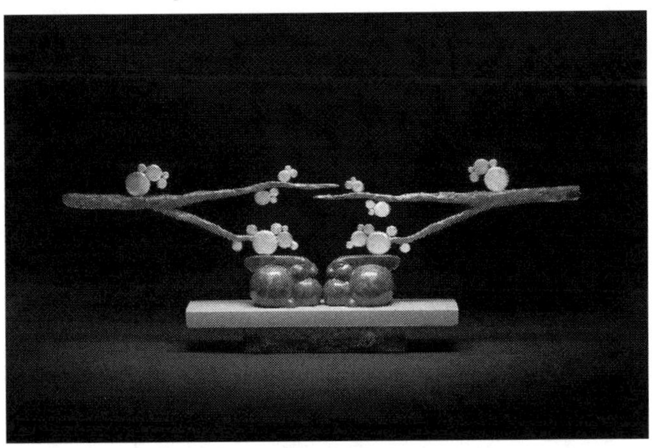

FIGURE 9 Tim Cherry, *Aspen Undercover*, Bronze, 9″ H × 23″ W × 3″ D. 2023 *Prix de West Invitational Art Exhibition & Sale.*

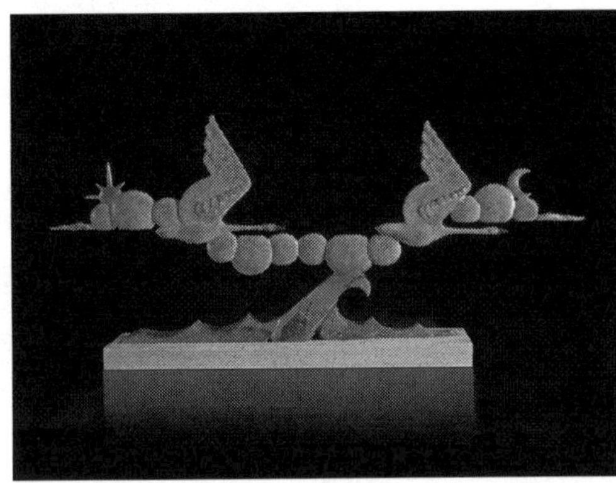

FIGURE 10 Tim Cherry, *Migration*, Bronze, 16″ H × 36″ W × 5″ D. 2023 *Prix de West Invitational Art Exhibition & Sale.*

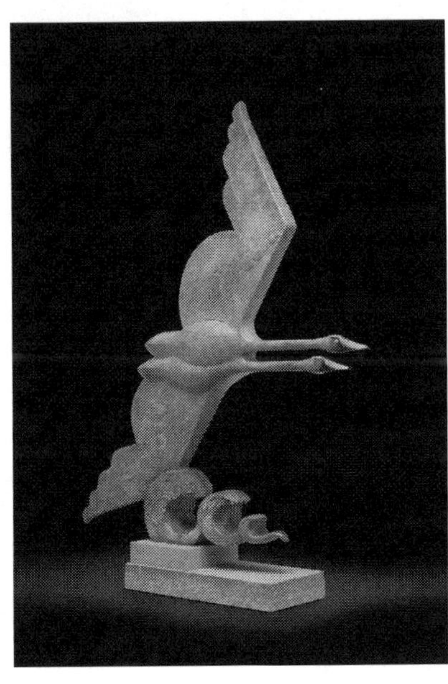

FIGURE 11 Tim Cherry, *Against the Wind*, Bronze, 55″ H × 44″ W × 10″ D. 2023 *Prix de West Invitational Art Exhibition & Sale.*

exhibition catalog, Buswell stated that it "captures that moment in time, after the rodeo clown has done his job of diverting the bull's attention away from the fallen rider, when he suddenly realizes the bull's focus is now on *him*!"

Tim Cherry, *Against the Wind*
Major General and Mrs Don D. Pittman Wildlife Award

Having participated in *Prix de West* for 27 consecutive years, Branson, Missouri, based sculptor Tim Cherry spent several years in the Yukon and Northwest Territories of his native Canada as a fishing and hunting guide and taxidermist before the age of 20 years. The firsthand knowledge of wildlife he gained during that time has informed his artwork ever since (Figures 9 and 10).

A fellow of the National Sculpture Society, Cherry's distinctive sculptures utilize simplified shapes and lines, as well as colorful patinas, to depict grace and movement in the creatures he portrays. At the 2001 *Prix de West*, Cherry was recipient of the James Earle Fraser Sculpture Award. In 2023, he was awarded the Major General and Mrs. Don D. Pittman Wildlife Award—which is given annually at *Prix de West* for exceptional artistic merit for a wildlife painting or sculpture—for his bronze *Against the Wind* (Figure 11).

"Swans are dedicated to each other through their lifetime," Cherry said in describing his *Against the Wind*, a bronze depiction of two swans in paired flight. "The pair in *Against the Wind* are fighting to move forward despite the headwinds of life in front of them. I wanted to show the pair in tandem,

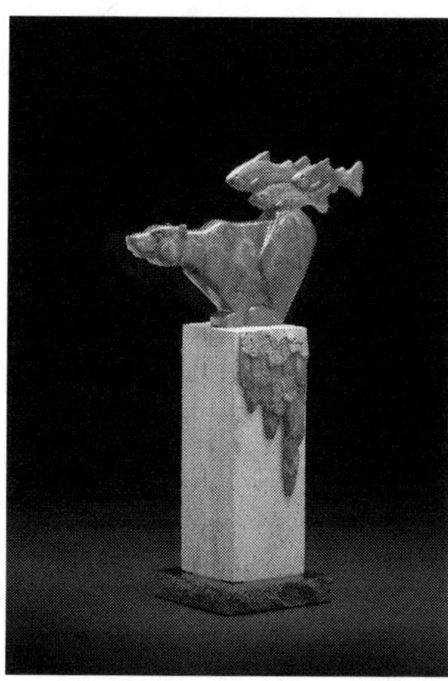

FIGURE 12 Tim Cherry, *Dreams of Salmon*, Bronze, 13″ H × 8″ W × 3″ D. 2023 *Prix de West Invitational Art Exhibition & Sale*.

working together as one for a common goal. From a distance, I want the viewer to see just one wingspan to represent the tightness, bond and unity of a couple."

Although *Prix de West* is a proudly Western art exhibition, the themes, concerns, hopes, and dreams reflected in the artwork there are universal. That's because, at its heart, the story of the West is the story of people from all walks of life, meaning that in each of us resides a little piece of the West (Figure 12).

Make plans now to attend the 52nd annual Prix de West Invitational Art Exhibition & Sale at the National Cowboy & Western Heritage Museum in Oklahoma City. The exhibition is open through August 4, 2024, with the Art Sale Weekend, including the fixed-price art sale, celebrations, a silent auction, and seminars, including a special demonstration by John Coleman, June 7–8, 2024. For more information about the 2024 *Prix de West*, visit https://pdw.nationalcowboymuseum.org/.

Received: 10 April 2024 | Accepted: 10 May 2024

DOI: 10.1002/smo3.12001

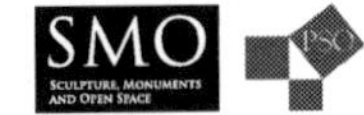

ARTICLE

Legal protection for visual artists

B.D. Kerrick

Correspondence
B.D. Kerrick
Email: songmayl@gmail.com

Abstract

It is essential that sculptors, architects, and other three-dimensional artists gain some familiarity with the extent and limits of intellectual property (IP) law and how it protects visual artists and their works. The main areas of IP legal protection for artists are traditional copyright law, the Visual Artists Rights Act, and the Architectural Works Copyright Protection Act. This article attempts to distill the large and complex discipline of intellectual property rights for visual artists. Legislative bodies, courts, nongovernmental organizations, international and intergovernmental institutions, and IP experts continue to struggle with the question of how to balance the public-good benefits of legal protection for artists with the demands of commerce. From copyrights to courts to alternative resolutions and other interventions, IP is a discipline broad and intricate, but visual artists have many options, including legal, organizational, and educational opportunities, to strengthen their position.

KEYWORDS

artist, copyright, sculpture, visual art

1 | INTRODUCTION

It is essential that sculptors, architects, and other three-dimensional artists gain some familiarity with the extent and limits of intellectual property (IP) law and how it protects visual artists and their works. The main areas of IP legal protection for artists are traditional copyright law, the Visual Artists Rights Act, and the Architectural Works Copyright Protection Act.

This article attempts to provide a digest of IP law for visual artists and does not constitute legal advice. If you have a specific issue, please seek the advice of a qualified attorney.

1.1 | Works of visual art

US copyright law[1] defines visual art for the purpose of determining a work's eligibility for copyright according to the attributes of a given work of art. Other works listed as not eligible for copyright as visual art may be copyrightable under other parts of copyright law.

The law describes a work of visual art as "a painting, drawing, print, or sculpture, existing in a single copy, or in a limited edition of 200 copies or fewer that are signed and consecutively numbered by the author (the term author refers to artists too—see below), or, in the case of a sculpture, in multiple cast, carved, or fabricated sculptures of 200 or fewer that are consecutively numbered by the author and bear the signature or other identifying mark of the author."[2]

A work of art of more than 200 copies is considered to be art of a commercial nature. Commercial art is made with the primary purpose of selling or promoting things, whereas visual art is created for the sake of esthetics or contemplation.[3]

Art produced for the primary sake of commerce had been determined by law not to be copyrightable, until 2017 when the Supreme Court substantially challenged that determination.[4] The case in that ruling will be explored below. Recently, relying on interpretations of existing law, both the courts and the US Copyright Office (Figure 1) have opined that artwork generated by artificial intelligence without guidance by a human being is not eligible for copyright.[5]

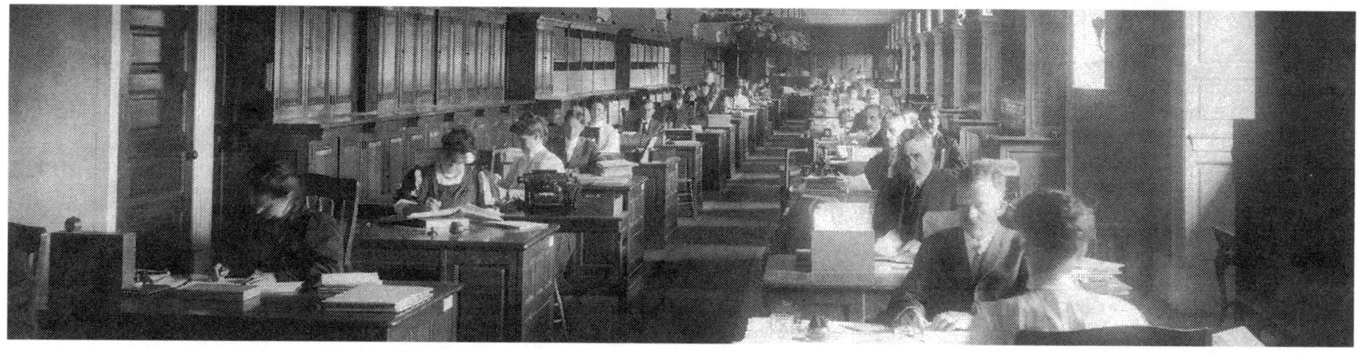

FIGURE 1 The US Copyright Office in the first Library of Congress Building, later named the Thomas Jefferson Building in 1980. The Office was moved to the John Adams Building and is currently in the James Madison Memorial Building, all L.O.C. buildings. A Copyright Office spokesperson confirmed to this writer the Office and its location and the date of the photo as circa 1920.

1.2 | Pictorial, graphic, and sculptural works

The statutory phrase "pictorial, graphic, and sculptural works" has a broader meaning than "works of visual art," and refers to "two-dimensional and three-dimensional works of fine, graphic, and applied art, photographs, prints and art reproductions, maps, globes, charts, diagrams, models, and technical drawings, including architectural plans."

1.3 | Intellectual property

Intellectual property has a still broader scope than copyright of pictorial, graphic, and sculptural works, and even copyright in general. IP refers to products of the mind that may have commercial value and include not only artistic works, but also many other works of the mind, such as inventions. So called ideational creations like inventions are trademarked rather than copyrighted.[6]

1.4 | Copyright, ownership, and transfer

A copyright is a set of legal rights granted to creators automatically at the moment the creator fixes the work in a tangible medium.[7] Companies and other organizations and people besides the creator can also own copyrights through works for hire or by other means of conveyance,[8] including through transfers, such as via contracts, wills, and bequests, or in special situations by court action.

1.5 | Copyright term limits

How long copyright protection lasts on a work depends on when it was created; duration has grown in the United States since the nation's first copyright act in 1790 that offered 28 years, including the renewal term of a work. Periodically, copyright terms and renewals have been extended. Works fixed on or after the date of the latest extension of January 1, 1978 are recognized for the lifetime of the artist plus 70 years. Copyrights on works for hire last 95 years from publication or 120 years from fixation, whichever is shorter.

1.6 | Public domain

When the copyright of a work expires, it falls into the public domain, at which time any member of the public can use it freely and legally. All works that were copyrighted or published before 1929 have fallen into the public domain. These include, most famously, Steamboat Willie (Figure 2), the first iteration of the Mickey Mouse character. But subsequent iterations of Mickey Mouse remain under copyright protection, and also continue to retain trademark protection as long as the image is in active use by its owner, The Walt Disney Company.[9]

1.7 | A brief history of visual arts copyright law in the United States

Legal protection for artists in general was granted at the nascence of the nation, although painters, sculptors, and architects were not mentioned specifically. The purpose of copyright law, as set out in the US Constitution, is "to promote the Progress of Science and the useful Arts, by securing for limited Times to Authors and Inventors the exclusive Right to their respective Writings and Discoveries." In the Copyright Act of 1870, the US Congress first specified copyright protection for "painting[s], drawing[s], chromo[s], statue [s], statuary, and... models or designs intended to be perfected as works of the fine arts."[10]

The term "author" continues to be used in copyright legalese to refer to creators in the various arts, and the usage was clarified in the 1884 case involving unsanctioned lithograph copies of a famous

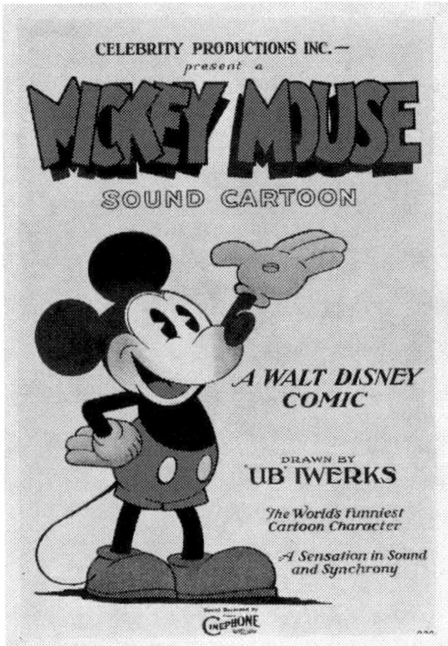

FIGURE 2 Mickey Mouse as Steamboat Willie in the eponymous black and white cartoon film of 1928. It was the first fully synchronized animated film. This original portrayal by Walt Disney and Ubbe Iwerks entered the public domain on 1 January, 2024, as did a color promotional poster for the film. Digital still print from the animated film. Wikimedia Commons. Public domain.

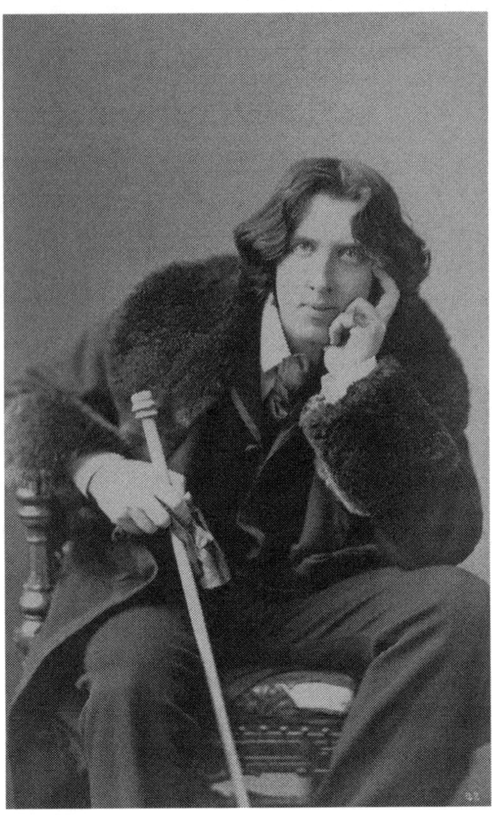

FIGURE 3 Oscar Wilde by Napoleon Sarony. Unauthorized lithographs of this print were challenged in Burrow-Giles Lithographic Company v. Sarony, 111 U.S. 53 (1884). Albumen print on card mount, sheet 30.6 × 18.4 cm, on mount 33 × 19 cm. Wikimedia Commons. Public domain.

photograph of Oscar Wilde (Figure 3). Throughout this article "author," "artist," and "creator" are used interchangeably.

Throughout the history of copyright, Congress and the courts have frequently reestablished the boundaries of copyright law in the arts. It was only by 1990 that Congress acted to extend explicit copyright protection to architectural works and added so-called moral rights for visual artists.[11]

1.8 | The civil law or moral rights concept of copyright

US copyright law is based on common law, such as that in other common law countries like the United Kingdom and Australia. Common law copyright is intended to provide an economic incentive to rights holders by granting them a monopoly on their individual works; whereas, civil law copyright, embraced by many more countries around the world, including those in Continental Europe, emphasizes the moral rights of the author.

The moral rights of the artist evolved from the philosophical concept of natural property rights, including "real" property, like land. Thus, by extension, moral rights protect the author's property of the mind.[12] In many countries these rights also provide protection for the author's dignity.

In addition to common law copyright in the United States, at the end of the last century, Congress finally added the moral rights of visual artists to the law, albeit more limited in scope than that found in civil law countries. These laws will be explored more fully below.

1.9 | Requirements of copyright

Over the last several decades there has been a trend away from formalities in copyright law. Before 1978, the word "copyright" or its symbol © had to be displayed on a published work and the work was to be registered with the US Copyright Office. In addition, copies had to be deposited with the Library of Congress. Now, under federal law, original and fixed works in one of the accepted categories of copyrightable subject matter receive automatic protection, as noted above. However, registration with the copyright office may provide substantially more monetary damages, and a copyright notice can serve to warn would-be infringers.

In the past, states were responsible for providing protection for unpublished works, but these works are now federally protected.

In the last 10 years or so, a few scholars and policy researchers have been calling for a return to some formalities. This is partly to address the dramatic rise in the last 25 years in "orphan works," that is, those works for which copyright owners cannot be located or contacted. Users cannot seek clearance from owners of orphan works, which subjects them to the risk of liability and causes other issues.[13]

Copyrightable subject matter as listed in Title 17 of the US Code,[14] Section 102, and which is within the purview of this article, includes pictorial, graphic, sculptural, and architectural works.

1.10 | Physical separability

According to the concept of physical separability, when a design can be physically separated from a useful object, the design, but not the useful aspects of the object, can be copyrighted. A lamp base design (Figure 4) was the subject of the US Supreme Court case, Mazer v. Stein, in 1954,[15] that added some clarity to the separability concept. The fact that the lamp base could be esthetically appreciated if the useful parts, such as the wire, socket, and harp, were removed qualified the base for copyright protection.

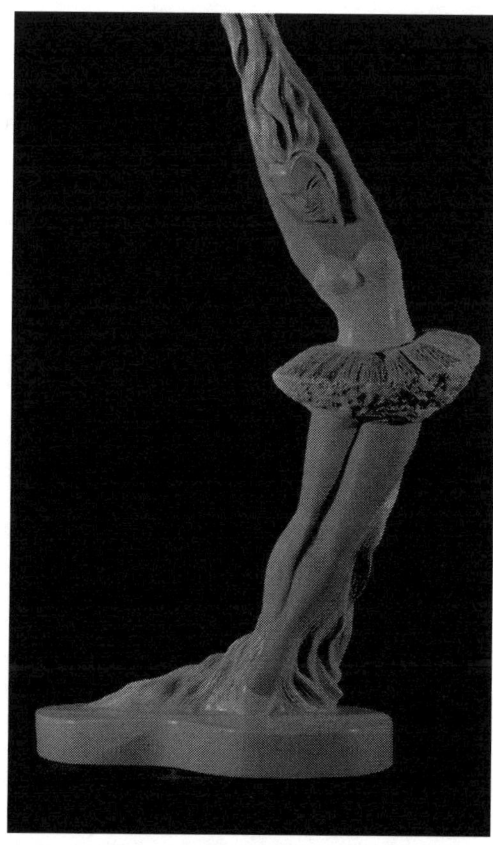

FIGURE 4 The statuette or statuettes in Mazer v Stein were vaguely referenced and not definitively described. The image shown, Curved Ballet Dancer—Female, H 1723, July 15, 1949, may be the one, or one of a few of, but, in any case, certainly representative of, the Stein statuettes in the dispute, and also fits the description in one of several similar court cases involving Stein's statuette lamp bases. The bases were made of semivitreous china. Public domain.

1.11 | Conceptual separability

Conceptual separability is a concept wherein the design of an object cannot be physically separated normally, but can be *conceived* to be separate.

1.12 | Merger of physical and conceptual separability

In the 2017 case of Star Athletica, LLC v. Varsity Brands,[16] Supreme Court Justice Clarence Thomas wrote the majority opinion that merged physical and conceptual separability. He wrote, "Because we reject the view that a useful article must remain after the artistic feature has been imaginatively separated from the article, we necessarily abandon the distinction between 'physical' and 'conceptual' separability. [...] We hold that an artistic feature of the design of a useful article is eligible for copyright protection if the feature (1) can be perceived as a two- or three-dimensional work of art separate from the useful article and (2) would qualify as a protectable pictorial, graphic, or sculptural work either on its own or in some other medium if imagined separately from the useful article."

1.13 | Idea—expression dichotomy

Only a particular expression of an idea can be copyrighted, not the idea itself. Bleistein v Donaldson Lithographing Co.,[17] in 1903, addressed that and other important aspects of copyright protection in a work of visual art. Donaldson made exact reproductions of three original Bleistein lithographs of a circus advertisement for The Great Wallace Shows (Figure 5).

The idea of circus performers gracing a lithograph was held not copyrightable, but the expression, that is, the particular arrangement of the performers, their poses, and so forth taken as a whole and as fixed in a medium was found to be so. Justice Oliver Wendell Holmes, Jr., writing for the majority opined that "others are free to copy the original," referring to the imagining or actual arrangement, poses, and appearance of the performers. "They are not free to copy the copy," that is, to reproduce the initial poster. This comment also highlights originality as an important distinction in eligibility for copyright.

1.14 | Originality, copyrightable subject matter, and fixation; the three central tenets of copyright

There are three central tenets of copyright law. As the fundament of these, *originality* does not necessarily mean novel or innovative. It means that an author

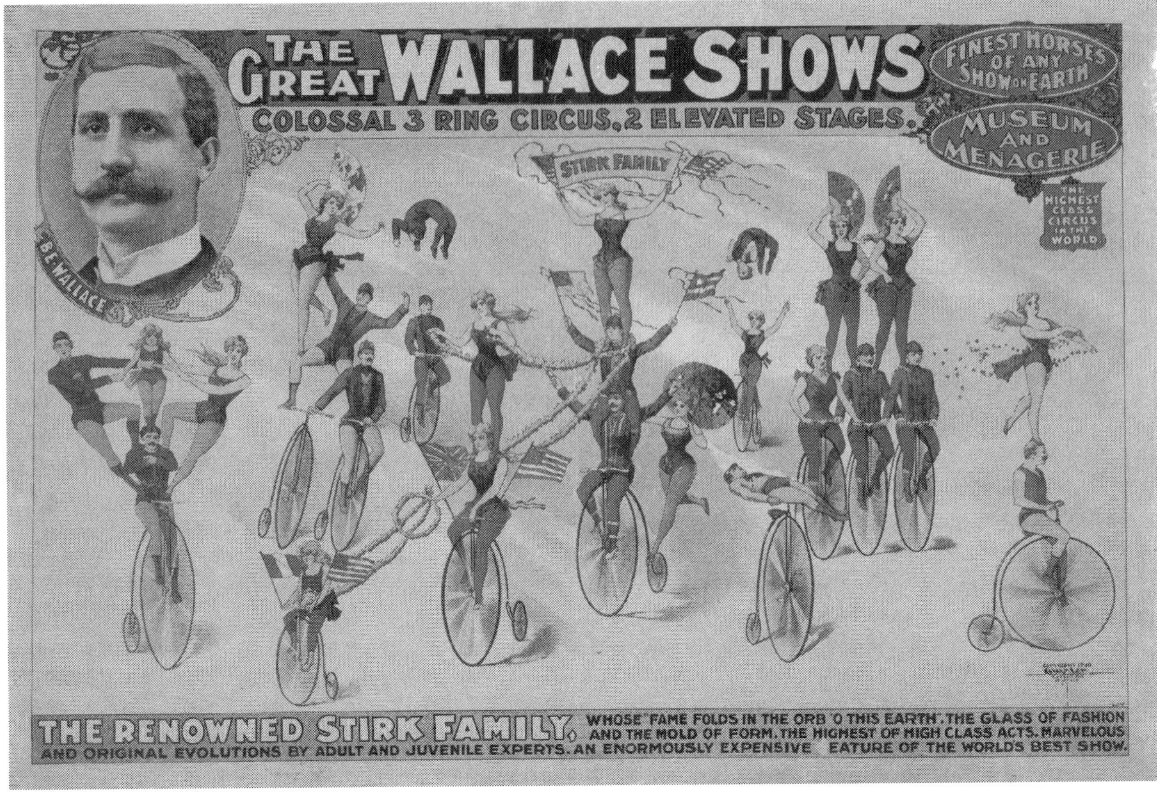

FIGURE 5 One of the lithograph posters of "The Great Wallace Shows" circus, depicting "the renowned Stirk Family." Additional lithographs printed by Donaldson, who was not the original printer, were disputed in Bleistein v Donaldson Lithographing Co., 188 U.S. 239 (1903). Wikimedia Commons. Public domain.

conceived a work without knowledge of whether a substantially similar work by another person exists and, therefore, the author did not copy the work.[18] One wording by the Supreme Court is, "originality necessitates independent creation plus a modicum of creativity."[19]

As to judging what constitutes creativity, Justice Holmes argued in the Bleistein case that "[i]t would be a dangerous undertaking for persons trained only to the law to constitute themselves final judges of the worth of [a work], outside of the narrowest and most obvious limits." In the 2023 case of Warhol v. Goldsmith,[20] Justice Sonia Sotomayor wrote for the majority of the Supreme Court in affirming that standard. The modicum of creativity is a naggingly nebulous concept for which the courts have not been able to set clear guidelines.[21]

Another of the tenets is that a work must be a *copyrightable subject matter* that has been specifically listed in the US Code. Included are creative works like paintings and sculpture and excluded are noncreative works like phone books and ledger books.

Fixation is the last of the three basic tenets of copyright. As described above, for fixation to occur, a work cannot be merely an idea, but must be "fixed in a tangible medium of expression," and for longer than a "transitory duration."[22]

1.15 | Bundle of exclusive rights

A copyright owner, which is usually the author, is entitled to a monopoly on a bundle of exclusive rights. These include the right to reproduce the work, to prepare derivative works (such as a photograph of a three-dimensional work), to display the work, and to distribute copies to the public (sell, rent, etc.), subject to the First Sale Doctrine.

The First Sale Doctrine allows the owner of a lawful copy (as in the purchaser of a statue), without authorization by the copyright owner, to sell or otherwise transfer ownership of the copy or to display that copy (such as within a home, office, or museum). But the owner of said copy must get authorization from the copyright holder to display the copy in a different medium, for instance, on television, film, or online.

However, some actions are exceptional to this right. For example, where an artist has authorized display of a work online in the United States, the work thus being viewed online from within a foreign country does not constitute infringement.

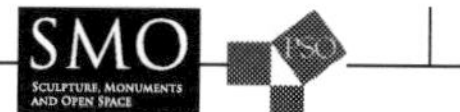

1.16 | Copyright infringement versus fair use

Infringement occurs when any one or more of the bundle of rights is exploited without the authorization of the copyright holder and therefore results in breaking the holder's monopoly. However, the fair use doctrine limits the monopoly afforded to the artist. It allows for the limited use of a copyrighted work without need for authorization by the copyright holder, including the use of copies for the purposes of criticism, comment, news reporting, teaching, scholarship, or research. But a court must consider a few factors to decide whether a use constitutes infringement or fair use.

1.17 | The four fair use factors

In 17 U.S.C. § 107 the fair use factors that allow someone to use a holder's work are enumerated as follows. Determinations to be made are:

1. The purpose and character of the use, including whether such use is of a commercial nature or is for nonprofit educational purposes,
2. The nature of the copyrighted work,
3. The amount and substantiality of the portion used in relation to the copyrighted work as a whole and,
4. The effect of the use upon the potential market for or value of the copyrighted work.

These factors are considered even for an unpublished work.

1.17.1 | First factor: Transformative use

In the first factor, to be considered, in addition to the commercial versus nonprofit educational use, is whether a use of a work transforms or only repackages the original. As Pierre N. Leval a prominent Judge explained in an influential article in Harvard Law Review, the original matter must be “transformed in the creation of new information, new esthetics, new insights and understandings—this is the very type of activity that the fair use doctrine intends to protect for the enrichment of society.”[23] He adds that other forms of transformation may include criticism of the original, parody, symbolism, and other uses. A court may also decide whether a respondent to a complaint acted in good faith, such as, with right intention rather than with malice.

1.17.2 | Second factor: Reuse

The second factor applies to the nature of the copyrighted work. In particular, the doctrine of fair use is applied more forgivingly toward the reuse of a published work than an unpublished work, and a factual work more than a fictional one.

1.17.3 | Third factor: Substantiality

The third factor of the doctrine of fair use applies to the amount of the original work that is used in the new one and the substantiality, or real worth and importance, of the portion used.

1.17.4 | Fourth factor: Market effect

The fourth factor covers the effect of the use upon the potential market for, or value of, the copyrighted work.

1.18 | Important cases of fair use

1.18.1 | *Rogers v. Koons*

In an influential case, Rogers v. Koons,[24] Jeff Koons was accused of unauthorized appropriation of a photograph taken by professional photographer Art Rogers. Koons rendered a sculpture, *String of Puppies,* nearly identical to Rogers' photo *Puppies*. He had altered the scene somewhat by placing daisies in the hair of the couple and elsewhere, painting the puppies blue, and altering the noses of the puppies.

Koons argued for fair use because the work is a parodic comment on the banality of everyday scenes in life. But the opinion of the court was that Koons could have expressed parody without copying the specific image. The court also held the artist liable for infringement as the similarity was substantial and that he had possessed the photograph. Furthermore, Koons had torn the copyright notice from Roger's original photographic print before turning it over to his sculpture team, thus demonstrating malice, in the legal sense of the term. The court decided that Koons had failed all four of the fair-use factors.

1.18.2 | *Campbell v. Acuff-Rose*

Campbell v. Acuff-Rose Music, Inc.,[25] was a dispute involving two music recordings, but the question of fair use at the heart of the case also applies to the visual arts. Rap group 2 Live Crew (aka The 2 Live Crew) used the titular lyric line and associated melodic line along with the famous guitar and bass riff from Roy Orbison's 1964 hit “Oh, Pretty Woman” in a recording of their own titled “Pretty Woman.” The US Supreme Court in 1990 unanimously held that the two Live Crew parody was fair use.

Unlike Koons, Luther Campbell, who wrote the rap adaptation, convinced the court that his work was a parody because it added "something new, with further purpose or different character by altering the original with new expression, meaning, or message." The court added that transformative works such as this are the "fair use doctrine's guarantee of breathing space within the confines of copyright." Furthermore, the court held that commercial use of an original does not undermine a fair use defense.

1.18.3 | *Blanch v. Koons*

Another case involving Koons, Blanch v. Koons,[26,27] in 2006, again dealt with questions of fair use. Andrea Blanch had produced a photograph titled *Silk Sandals by Gucci* for Allure magazine, which showed a woman's sandal-adorned feet supinely resting on a man's lap. Jeff Koons used a computer to scan the feet and legs, and, having removed the original background, rotated them to appear dangling and incorporated the image into a painting titled *Niagara* that shows three other pairs of legs and feet.

The Court held that the painting was transformative in that Blanch's photograph was "banal" whereas Koons' painting was creative. "The amount and substantiality of the portion used in relation to the copyrighted work as a whole" was ruled insignificant. The market for the Koons painting was not the same market as Blanch's image that was used as an advertisement in a magazine, therefore, the painting did not impact the potential market for the photograph.

1.18.4 | *Cariou v. Prince*

Patrick Cariou published *Yes Rasta*, a book of photographs depicting natural scenery and portraits in Jamaica. Appropriation artist Richard Prince bought several copies of the book and clipped and incorporated several of the photographs into a series of collages and paintings. He exhibited the resultant series of 30 pieces named Canal Zone at a gallery.

Cariou sued the painter for infringement and the court took his side. In the 2013 case Cariou v Prince, the court held that to qualify for a fair use defense, the work of appropriation must "comment on, relate to the historical context of, or critically refer back to the original works."

However, Prince appealed and the Court of Appeals[28] reversed the lower court's decision. The Court of Appeals held that the work need not comment on the original to be considered transformative. The court found that the 25 out of the total 30 works qualified for a fair use defense. Those works were transformative because Prince's "composition, presentation, scale, color palette, and media are fundamentally different and new compared to the photographs, as is the expressive nature of Prince's work."

The court concluded that the paintings did not impact the market for the photographer's works. The five remaining works, however, because of their extraordinary similarity to the originals, did not fit the standard for fair use and the disputants eventually settled on those out of court.

1.19 | Conclusion on fair use findings in visual art cases

The courts historically have struggled with the ambiguity and uncertainty of fair use. Many fair use cases have zigzagged up the appeals process for and against particular findings, demonstrating the difficulty of predicting the outcome of a case of fair use in such a subjective field as the arts.

1.20 | The Visual Artists Rights Act and the Berne Convention

The US Congress passed the Visual Artists Rights Act of 1990 (VARA) to complement and incorporate into the Copyright Act. It was passed in an effort to bring the US closer in compliance with the Berne Convention for the Protection of Literary and Artistic Works.

Berne, established in 1886, informed the civil law tradition in Europe and around the world, particularly with regard to *droits moral,* or moral rights in English. In the singular form droit moral refers to an artist's innate right to control the future of one's works.[29]

Berne also introduced the lack-of-formality concept into copyright law, eliminating the requirements for registration and copyright notice. The Convention requires that member countries recognize the copyright laws of all other member countries. All but a handful of countries in the world are members of Berne. The World Intellectual Property Organization (WIPO)[30] administers Berne along with over two dozen other international intellectual property treaties.

1.20.1 | VARA: Specific moral rights

With VARA the United States finally recognized the moral rights of artists, but to a more limited extent than most other countries. While Berne applies moral rights to a comprehensive variety of creatives, VARA limits moral rights to visual artists. With both Berne and VARA, legal remedies to redress violations of moral rights remain spectacularly unique to visual artists.[31]

Representative Edward Markey was a major supporter and sponsor of the VARA legislation, along with the strong backing of Senator Edward Kennedy. Markey said, "Artists in this country play a very important role in capturing the essence of the culture and recording it for future generations."[32]

1.20.2 | Berne: Specific moral rights

Berne and civil law countries in general also offer a more extensive set of moral rights protections to artists than does VARA.[33] These include the right to be credited for one's work, to protect the Integrity of one's work, to decide when to publish a work, to expect a work to be returned upon demand, to have one's dignity protected, such as from excessive criticism, and to be reimbursed if the work is resold.[34]

1.20.3 | VARA: Attribution and integrity rights

VARA, as embodied in the code, lists the attribution and integrity rights of visual artists,[35] and these rights are subject to the fair use limitations described above. The code says that the author shall have the right to claim authorship of a particular work; the author can prevent the use of one's name as the author of a work that one did not create, or can prevent the use of one's name in the event of distortion, mutilation, or other modification of the work which would harm one's honor or reputation; the author has the right to prevent any actual intentional distortion, mutilation, or other modification of a work; and can, in the case of a work of "recognized stature," prevent any intentional or grossly negligent destruction of that work.

1.21 | Limitations on moral rights

The code lists exceptions to the right to prevent modification, for example, modifications caused by the passage of time, the inherent nature of the materials, the result of conservation, or of public presentation, such as, lighting or placement.

To protect the author from the unfair power balance that often occurs in negotiations with a client,[36] the code specifies that the moral rights of the author are independent of the copyrights of the author's individual works, and these rights may not be transferred. The author may waive these rights, however, and only in writing.

1.22 | Criticism of VARA

VARA has many critics. Some claim the act goes too far and stifles the free flow of commerce, and others say it needs to be strengthened. Critics also would like to see the language clarified as to what works of art qualify for "recognized stature."[37]

1.23 | The architectural works copyright protection act

The courts have long considered architectural plans, blueprints, and models as copyrightable, although they were not specifically mentioned in the copyright acts in the United States and the rights were not vigorously enforced. Besides, architects traditionally have preferred to depend on the reputations of their peers as their guarantee of protection of their designs.[38]

Eventually, the Architectural Works Copyright Protection Act of 1990 (AWCPA), was passed by Congress at the time of VARA, and right after the United States joined Berne. The stated purpose was to "stimulate excellence in design, thereby enriching our public environment in keeping with the constitutional goal." Like VARA, AWCPA was incorporated into copyright law.[39]

1.24 | The range of rights permitted for architectural works

Architectural Works share only some of the protections afforded sculptural works. For instance, AWCPA extends protections only to free standing, habitable structures. Monuments, are the exception. Although they are not buildings, monuments are protected as both sculptures and architectural works.

An architect whose architectural work has been constructed is not afforded the right to prevent anyone else from making, distributing, or publicly displaying pictures, paintings, photographs, or other pictorial representations of the work, if the building in which the work is embodied is located in, or is ordinarily visible from, a public space. In addition, an architect may not prevent the owners of a building from altering or destroying the building.[40]

However, the architect has one distinct advantage in the relationship with a building owner. The architect remains the owner of the copyright, but the owner or contractor of the building is only granted a nonexclusive license to use the plans for that project.[41] Therefore, the architect maintains the exclusive right to create adaptations or modifications of the work.[42]

1.25 | Historically significant buildings are not necessarily safe from destruction

Laws in place including at the federal level do not always prevent the destruction of important and historical buildings, especially their interiors. A case in

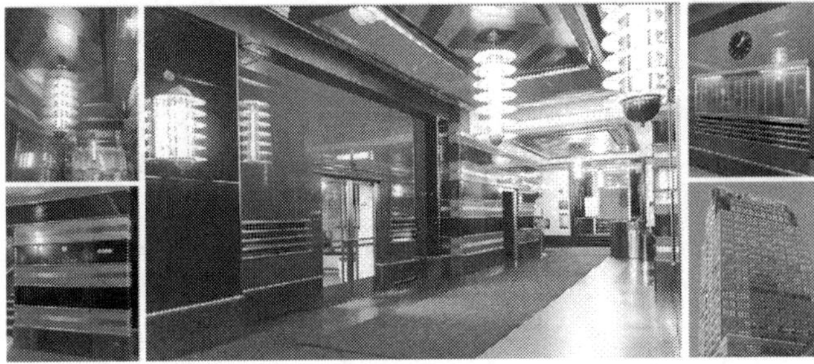

FIGURE 6 The original Streamline Moderne lobby of the McGraw-Hill building. This set of photographs was used by the Art Deco Society of New York on gopetition.com in 2021 as part of efforts to preserve the lobby. Photographs reprinted by special permission of Lynn Farrell, lynnfarrellphotography.com.

point is the lobby of the McGraw-Hill building in New York City (Figure 6). Art critics and architecture preservationists regarded it as one of the world's last great interiors from the Streamline Moderne period of the Art Deco era.[43]

The building was completed in 1931 with the exterior receiving landmark status from the New York City Landmarks Preservation Commission (LPC) in 1979 while the interior did not. This was regardless of arguments such as one by the Art Deco Society of New York that design elements "at the main entrance are seamlessly carried into the lobby."[44]

In 2021, preservationist Lloyd Bergenson discovered and raised the alarm about a proposal by architects in charge of renovating the building to replace the lobby with a radically different design.[45]

Mr. Bergenson and other prominent preservationists formed an alliance[46] to persuade and ultimately sue the LPC but the courts rejected their efforts.[47]

1.26 | Alternatives to infringement litigation

Congress passed the Copyright Alternative in Small Claims Enforcement Act (CASE) in 2020, which established a small claims court called the Copyright Claims Board (CCB)[48] that copyright holders can use to pursue damages[49] up to US$15,000 per work infringed and US$30,000 per proceeding, not including attorneys' fees and costs that may be awarded separately.[50]

1.26.1 | Alternative dispute resolution (ADR)

Other cheaper but worthy alternatives to litigation, collectively called ADR,[51] include mediation or arbitration or even a promise to make a good faith effort to communicate with each other before starting a formal action.[52] A dispute resolution clause can be added to a contract between an independent contractor and a client by mutual agreement.[53]

1.26.2 | Mediation

Although a disputant could be at a disadvantage without a skilled attorney present, mediation does offer advantages over litigation. These can include privacy, confidentiality, and informality, and can be nonbinding. A trained third-party neutral mediates the dispute. Mediation can save time and expense and may preserve relationships.

1.26.3 | Arbitration

Arbitration is more formal than mediation, but likewise offers advantages over litigation, including privacy and confidentiality. Arbitration is decided by a neutral third-party comprising one or three arbitrators, and the process can be binding if the clause in a contract spells that out. Arbitration usually saves more time and money than litigation but not as much as mediation.

Critics charge that arbitration clauses violate a party's right to due process in court. A disputant disappointed in the outcome of the arbitration could argue that the arbitration clause is invalid, and if successful, could have the findings of the arbitration invalidated. To mitigate the possibility of such a challenge, language in the contract could be drawn in such a way as to maintain the option to turn to the courts.

1.27 | Alternatives to copyright

Alternatives to Copyright that are available to visual artists include Creative Commons (CC)[54] and alternative compensation systems (ACS),[55] such as a threshold pledge system (examples are Kickstarter and Patreon), and are touted as effective means to redress perceived weaknesses in the current copyright regime, especially with regard to its monopoly-based compensation and enforcement schemes.

A radical, new ACS being proposed is The Artistic Freedom Voucher. As with several other non-government systems, it depends upon government intervention to be effective.

1.28 | CC

CCs licenses likewise do not replace copyright, yet, so far, they have proven to be enforceable.[56] Its several licenses provide standardized releases or waivers of certain restrictions as permitted by copyright law and thereby obviate negotiations between an artist and a buyer or other consumer of one's individual works.

All CC licenses require a minimum standard for licensees, which is to provide attribution to the artist, denoted on a CC notice as BY, when the work is used and if it is shared. CC offers three more license types to integrate with BY, and the four types combine to form a total of six licenses.

Combined with BY the othet types are "NonCommercial" (NC), "NoDerivatives" (ND), and "ShareAlike" (SA). SA requires that adaptations of the work be released under the same license as the original work.[57]

1.29 | Monitoring for, and protecting against, infringement of artists' works

An internet service provider is not legally obligated to monitor its service for copyright infringement from bad actors,[58] so it is up to the artist to patrol the internet for possible acts of infringement. Online monitor and alert services for visual artists, like ATO Platform,[59] and more generally for all content, Google Alerts,[60] are available to artists. Alternatively, artists may choose to limit potential infringement by reducing the quality of, or altering, or obfuscating parts of image reproductions online. Examples include lowering the resolution, cropping the image, and superimposing a watermark.

1.30 | When litigation and ADR is cost prohibitive

A simple intervention is to send a cease and desist notice to an infringer—however, having an attorney send the notice on the law firm's stationery might be more effective than an artist sending it independently.

Artists rights organizations like the Artists Rights Society[61] offer information and guidance on copyright and licensing and, with membership, even a service that monitors unauthorized uses of artists' works.[62]

Pro bono and reduced-fee law organizations across the United States and across the world provide legal services to artists and arts organizations. Volunteer Lawyers for the Arts–New York[63] has posted on their website a free directory of organizations far and wide that are similar to their own.[64]

1.31 | The future of legal protections for creatives

Inventions throughout history like the printing press, lithography, and peer-to-peer internet have disrupted legal and technical protection schemes of creatives, and now three-dimension printing and artificial intelligence pose and presage challenges to current protections.

2 | CONCLUSION

This article attempts to distill the large and complex discipline of intellectual property rights for visual artists. Legislative bodies, courts, nongovernmental organizations, international and intergovernmental institutions, and IP experts continue to struggle with the question of how to balance the public-good benefits of legal protection for artists with the demands of commerce. From copyrights to courts to alternative resolutions and other interventions, IP is a discipline broad and intricate, but visual artists have many options, including legal, organizational, and educational opportunities, to strengthen their position.[65]

ENDNOTES

1 17 U.S.C. § 101.

2 U.S. Copyright Office, Copyright Law of the United States, (Title 17), Chapter 1: Subject Matter and Scope of Copyright, § 101 definitions. https://copyright.gov/title17/92chap1.html.

3 Spacey, John, 11 Types of Commercial Art, *Simplicable*, 2017 Apr 13. https://simplicable.com/culture/types-of-commercial-art.

4 Star Athletica, LLC v. Varsity Brands, Inc., No. 15-866, 580 U.S._ (2017), Appendix to the Opinion. https://www.supremecourt.gov/opinions/16pdf/15-866_0971.pdf.

5 Gomez, Martin, 172 Analyses of this statute by attorneys, Is It Possible to Copyright Works That Include AI-Generated Material? Casetext, Section 101—Definitions, *Goodwin Law,* 2023 Oct 4. https://www.goodwinlaw.com/en/insights/publications/2023/10/insights-technology-aiml-is-it-possible-to-copyright-works.

6 What is Intellectual Property? *World Intellectual Property Organization* (WIPO). https://www.wipo.int/about-ip/en/.

7 17 U.S.C. Ch 1: Subject Matter and Scope of Copyright, § 102. (a) Subject matter of copyright: In general. https://copyright.gov/title17/title17.pdf.

8 17 U.S.C. § 202(d).

9 Ulaby, Neda, 'Steamboat Willie' is now in the public domain. What does that mean for Mickey Mouse? NPR, *Morning Edition,* January 1, 2024. https://www.npr.org/2024/01/01/1221606624/mickey-mouse-public-domain-disney/.

10 Brauneis, Robert, Understanding Copyright's First Encounter With the Fine Arts: A Look at the Legislative History of the Copyright Act of 1870 (2020). Case Western Reserve Law Review, Vol. 71, No. 2, 2020, GWU Legal Studies Research Paper No. 2022-09, GWU Law School Public Law Research Paper No. 2022-09, Available at SSRN: https://ssrn.com/abstract=3942025.

11 A Brief History of Copyright in the United States, Copyright Office. https://www.copyright.gov/timeline.

12 *Ohio State University Libraries,* The Ohio State University Copyright Corner, Theories of Copyright, Personality Theory, 2014 May 9. https://library.osu.edu/site/copyright/2014/05/09/theories-of-copyright/.

13 Pallante, Maria, Orphan Works & Mass Digitization: Obstacles & Opportunities, Berkeley Tech. Law Journal, Vol. 27, Issue 3

(Symposium 2012). https://btlj.org/2012/01/volume-27-issue-3-symposium-2012-2/.

[14] U.S.C. of the House of Representatives, Office of the Law Revision Counsel of the United States House of Representatives. https://uscode.house.gov/.

[15] Mazer v. Stein, 347 U.S. 201 (1954), *Justia*, U.S. Law, U.S. Code Law, U.S. Supreme Court, Opinions by Volume. https://supreme.justia.com/cases/federal/us/347/201/.

[16] Star Athletica, LLC v. Varsity Brands, Inc., No. 15-866, 580 U.S. _ (2017), Appendix to the Opinion. https://www.supremecourt.gov/opinions/16pdf/15-866_0971.pdf.

[17] Bleistein v Donaldson Lithographing Co., 188 U.S. 239 (1903), *Justia*, U.S. Law, U.S. Code Law, U.S. Supreme Court, Opinions by Volume. https://supreme.justia.com/cases/federal/us/188/239/.

[18] Copyright Basics, Originality, University of Michigan, *Research Guides*. https://guides.lib.umich.edu/copyrightbasics/copyrightability.

[19] Feist Publications, Inc. v. Rural Tel. Serv. Co., 499 U.S. 340 (1991), *Justia*, U.S. Law, U.S. Code Law, U.S. Supreme Court, Opinions by Volume, Volume 499. https://supreme.justia.com/cases/federal/us/499/340/.

[20] Andy Warhol Foundation for Visual Arts, Inc. v. Goldsmith, 598 U.S. (2023), *Justia*, U.S. Law, U.S. Case Law, U.S. Supreme Court, Opinions by Volume, Volume 598. https://supreme.justia.com/cases/federal/us/598/21-869/.

[21] Phalen, Mitzi S., How Much is Enough? The Search for a Standard of Creativity in Works of Authorship under Section 102(a) of the Copyright Act of 1976, 68 Neb. L. Rev. 1989. https://digitalcommons.unl.edu/nlr/vol68/iss3/6.

[22] "Fixed," U.S. Copyright Office, Copyright Law of the United States, (Title 17), Chapter 1: Subject Matter and Scope of Copyright, § 101. Definitions. https://www.copyright.gov/title17/92chap1.html.

[23] Leval, Pierre N. 1990. "Toward a Fair Use Standard." *Harvard Law Review* 103 (5): 1105–36. https://www.jstor.org/stable/1341457.

[24] Rogers v. Koons, 960 F.2d 301 (2d Cir. 1992), U.S. Copyright Office, Fair Use Index. https://www.copyright.gov/fair-use/summaries/rogers-koons-2dcir1992.pdf.

[25] Campbell v. Acuff-Rose Music, Inc. 510 U.S. 569 (1994) Library of Congress, U. S. Reports. https://www.loc.gov/item/usrep510569/.

[26] Blanch v. Koons, 467 F.3d 244 (2nd Cir. 2006), *Casebriefsco*, Casebrief. https://casebriefsco.com/casebrief/blanch-v-koons.

[27] Blanch v. Koons, 467 F.3d 244 (2006), *Google Scholar,* Case Law. https://scholar.google.com/scholar_case?case=3752630071472494999&hl=en&as_sdt=2006.

[28] Cariou v. Prince, 714 F.3d 694 (2d Cir. 2013), United States Circuit for the Court of Appeals, Docket #, 11-1197-cv, Patrick Cariou v. Richard Prince, et al. https://ww3.ca2.uscourts.gov/decision.

[29] Rosenblatt, Betsy, Moral Rights, What are moral rights? Moral Rights Basics, *Harvard Law School*. https://cyber.harvard.edu/property/library/moralprimer.html.

[30] *WIPO,* A Brief History. https://www.wipo.int/about-wipo/en/history.html.

[31] Sheehan, Kerry and Walsh, Kit, EFF Says No to So-Called "Moral Rights" Copyright Expansion, *Electronic Frontier Foundation,* March 30, 2017. https://www.eff.org/deeplinks/2017/03/eff-says-no-so-called-moral-rights-copyright-expansion.

[32] Moreno, Ana-Victoria, VARA Turns Thirty-One: How Amending the Visual Artists Rights Act of 1990 to Add Guiding Language Can Further Advance the Act's Purpose, 8 *Tex. A&M J. Prop.* L. 103, p. 21, 2022. https://scholarship.law.tamu.edu/journal-of-property-law/vol8/iss2/3/; https://doi.org/10.37419/JPL.V8.

[33] U.S. Copyright Office, Authors, Attribution, and Integrity: Examining Moral Rights in the United States. https://www.copyright.gov/policy/moralrights/.

[34] Meindertsma, Jessica, Rights Management Specialist at the Copyright Resources Center, Ohio State University, *The Ohio State University Libraries,* The Ohio State University Copyright Corner, Theories of Copyright. https://library.osu.edu/site/copyright/2014/05/09/theories-of-copyright/.

[35] 17 USC § 106 A: Rights of certain authors to attribution and integrity, Office of the Law Revision Counsel of the United States House of Representatives, U.S. Code, Title 17-Copyrights, Chapter 1-Subject Matter and Scope of Copyright, 2008 Jan 8. https://uscode.house.gov/view.xhtml?req=granuleid:USC-2007-title17-section106A&num=0&edition=2007.

[36] Moreno, Ana-Victoria, "[The artist's] goal is to get commissions and put their work out in the world, so they are often forced to agree to certain contract terms they would not otherwise agree to to secure a commission," p. 115.

[37] Ibid, pp. 121–126.

[38] Fischer III, William W., Visual and Architectural Works, *Harvard University,* Lectures on Copyright Law, The Subject Matter of Copyright. https://wilkins.law.harvard.edu/courses/CopyrightX2018/CopyX%20L3.6.mp4.

[39] 17 U.S.C. § 102(a).

[40] 17 U.S.C. § 120(a), (b). https://www.copyright.gov/title17/92chap1.html#120.

[41] Loulakis, Michael C. and McLaughlin, Lauren P., Are Copyright Protections Eroding for Design Professionals? *Civil Engineering Source*, American Society of Civil Engineers, October 25, 2023. https://www.asce.org/publications-and-news/civil-engineering-source/civil-engineering-magazine/article/2023/10/are-copyright-protections-eroding-for-design-professionals.

[42] 17 U.S.C.§106(2). https://www.copyright.gov/title17/92chap1.html#106.

[43] Bonanos, Christopher, Change Is Coming to the McGraw-Hill Building's Art Deco Lobby. Or Is It? *New York* magazine, February 12, 2021. https://www.curbed.com/2021/02/mcgraw-hill-building-art-deco-lobby-landmark-fight.html.

[44] Art Deco Society of New York, "Save the Art Deco Lobby of the McGraw-Hill Building!," *GoPetition. com,* February 9, 2021. https://www.gopetition.com/petitions/save-the-art-deco-lobby-of-the-mcgraw-hill-building.html.

[45] Gannon, Devin, "Preservationists fight to save the impressively-intact Art Deco lobby of the McGraw-Hill Building," *6sqft – New York City,* February 24, 2021. https://www.6sqft.com/preservationists-fight-to-save-the-impressively-intact-art-deco-lobby-of-the-mcgraw-hill-building/.

[46] Do_co, mo. mo__us ny/tristate. https://wp.docomomo-nytri.org/wp-content/uploads/2021/03/McGraw-Hill-Alliance-Letter-to-LPC-03.01.21.pdf.

[47] Docket Alarm, The alliance to save the McGraw Hill Lobby et al. v. The Landmarks Preservation Commission of the City of New York et al., 152750/2021, NY State, NY County, Supreme Court, March 18, 2021. http://ocr.docketalarm.com/cases/New_York_State_New_York_County_Supreme_Court/152750—2021/THE_ALLIANCE_TO_SAVE_THE_McGRAW_HILL_LOBBY_et_al_v._THE_LANDMARKS_PRESERVATION_COMMISSION_OF_THE_CITY_OF_NEW_YORK_et_al/.

[48] U.S. Copyright Office, Small Claims. https://www.copyright.gov/about/small-claims/.

[49] U.S. Copyright Office, Chapter 15, Copyright Small Claims: Permissible Remedies: Monetary Recovery, Actual Damages, Profits, and Statutory Damages for Infringement: Statutory Damages: "With respect to works timely registered," Legislative Developments, H.R. 133, bill excerpt (CASE Act), 17 U.S.C. § 1504 (e) (1) (A) (ii) (I) [p. 94].

[50] U.S. Copyright Office, Legislative Developments, H.R. 133, bill excerpt (CASE Act), Chapter 15, Copyright Small Claims: Permissible Remedies: Monetary Recovery, Limitation on Total Monetary Recovery, 17 U.S.C. § 1504 (e) (1) (A) [p95].

[51] Prowda, Judith B., "Esq, 15 min on the Mediation of Arts Related Disputes." *Stropheus Art Law.* https://youtu.be/gL9wKS1ECzc.

[52] Newburn, Ryan N., "Pros and Cons of Mediation vs Arbitration vs Litigation." *Newburn Law,* Legal Articles, August 16, 2022. https://www.newburnlaw.com/pros-and-cons-of-mediation-vs-arbitration-vs-litigation.

[53] Ibid.

[54] *Creative Commons.* https://creativecommons.org/.

[55] Copyright Alternatives, *Wikipedia.* https://en.m.wikipedia.org/wiki/Copyright_alternatives.

[56] Frequently Asked Questions. *Creative Commons.* https://creativecommons.org/faq/.

[57] What Are Creative Commons Licenses? *Creative Commons.* https://creativecommons.org/faq/#what-are-creative-commons-licenses.

[58] 17 U.S.C. § 512. https://www.copyright.gov/title17/92chap5.html#512.

[59] ATO Platform. https://atoplatform.com/.

[60] Alerts. *Google.* https://www.google.com/alerts.

[61] *ARSNY.* https://arsny.com/.

[62] *Artists Rights Society.* https://arsny.com/protect/resources/.

[63] *VLANY.* https://vlany.org/.

[64] *VLANY.* https://vlany.org/national-directory-of-volunteer-lawyers-for-the-arts/.

[65] All material referenced in the endnotes that are from online sources were accessed from November 2023 through May 2024.

Made in the USA
Columbia, SC
31 August 2024